Writing about the frontier
MARK TWAIN

This book is for my daughter Allison who one day will be able to reach a whole new world through the books of Mark Twain.

Bookshelf for Young Americans

Writing about the frontier

MARK TWAIN

by Jean Rikhoff

Illustrated by Richard Mlodock

Published by
KINGSTON HOUSE, *Chicago*

TABLE OF CONTENTS

Chapter *1*

Lost In A Cave

The candle flickered and sputtered. The little flame glittered in the darkness. All around the two children the darkness was like a big mouth, opening its jaws to swallow them. Sam Clemens held the candle high for Laura to see the shining ceiling of stalactites. The candle bobbed and died, sprang up again. There was hardly more than the length of a boy's thumb left to light their way back.

"Are we lost, Sam?" Laura asked in a frightened voice.

Sam was afraid to tell the truth. He thought of how the two of them had been safe with the rest of the picnic party less than an hour before. All the school children and a few adults—their chaperons—had started out joyously to explore the cave. Over the children's screams of delight and exclamations of awe, the adults had warned them again and again not to drift away. But Sam knew the cave. He was already savoring Laura's delight when he showed her a part of the cave none of the others would explore. He thought of how envious the other boys and girls would be when he and Laura returned and told of their adventures.

He had pulled Laura behind, whispering. "You want to see something special, something none of the others know about?"

Laura had looked around hesitantly. The cave was dark and cold, there were bats in some of the passages. She was afraid, Sam knew, but the last thing in the world she wanted to show was her fear.

They had stolen away from the party at one of the branching passages. They had a supply of candles and Sam was sure he knew the way. They started down a winding passage, holding the candle high and reading the names of people who had been there before them and scratched their names on the walls. Although most of the names were familiar, here and there was a strange one. Was it someone long ago who had put his name here and then left Hannibal to move West? Sam and Laura did not know, but they made up stories to go with the names.

In many places the walls of the cave were blackened by the smoke of other candles of long ago, and the passages had a dark, frightening look. But Sam confidently led the way. Wasn't he, Samuel Langhorne Clemens, the bravest boy in all of Hannibal, Missouri? And wasn't Laura Hawkins the prettiest girl in Hannibal? Sam felt proud to have the nicest girl in town relying on him. Well, he would show her underground lakes and places where he thought maybe there was buried treasure. He would take her to the "secret" room where his gang met.

"Are we lost, Sam?" Laura repeated, and Sam interrupted his reverie and looked around. They were lost all right, but he didn't want to say so.

"We'll just go a little further," he said confidently, "And then if we don't find this passage I'm looking for, we'll start back."

"I want to start back now," she said, stopping and clutching his hand. "I'm afraid."

He looked at her. Her lower lip was trembling and her eyes were filling with tears. "Now don't you cry," he said. "You just come a little way further and we'll—" But he did not know quite what they would do. A way back, that was all he kept hoping they would find. But nothing looked familiar.

At the end of the passage they came to a pool formed by water tumbling over a rock ledge and gathering in a wide cup in the floor. Sam wanted to cheer Laura up—he wanted to cheer himself up—and he placed the candle behind the falling water. The little shaft of light threw sparks of color on the water and reflected against the limestone ledge, which looked like a ruffle around the rim of the bright water. "Isn't it pretty?" he asked anxiously, trying to coax a smile from her.

"Let's go back," Laura said. "Let's turn around and go back." Then she looked earnestly at Sam. "You do know the way back, don't you, Sammy? We can go back, can't we?"

But Sam had forgotten his own fears. Behind the ledge of water he had discovered a natural rock stairway. "Look," he cried excitedly. "Look here what I found! Come on, let's explore." If there was one thing in the world Sam Clemens loved to do, it was to explore.

The children stumbled along the stairway, laughing and joking. Laura had forgotten her fears and was as excited as Sam. At the top of the stairway there was a large room, "like a cathedral," Sam said, remembering the pictures in his school books, and pleased at the admiring look that Laura gave him.

They crossed the wide floor of the inner cave and started down a passage which was lined with stalactites.

Groping fearfully through a maze of dark tunnels

At the bottom of the narrow tunnel there was a spring, and when Sam held up the candle, they saw a fairyland reflected in the water. The water rippled and shone as tiny drops fell from the ceiling; the stalactites were mirrored in the candlelit surface of the pool. The basin of the little lake was a glittering frostwork of crystals.

"It's just beautiful," Laura said at last. "I never saw anything so beautiful in my life. Let's go back and tell the others. I want them to come see."

Her voice was so determined that Sam knew there was nothing he could say to change her mind.

"Well," he said hesitantly, "Well—"

But Laura had already run up to him and was tugging at his hand. "Give me a candle, too," she said. "I want to look."

"I don't have too many more. There's just one," he said, feeling in his pocket. "Maybe we better save that."

"But we're going right back, we're—Sam Clemens," she said angrily, "you take me right back this minute." And she stamped her foot.

He nodded miserably and started back across the vast cavern. But there were three passages that opened out at the far end. He looked at Laura fearfully. "Do you remember which one we came in by?" he asked timidly.

"No, I don't," Laura said. "I think—I think it was this one, but—" At that moment a vast knot of bats shown in the candlelight. They were bunched together and hanging from the roof of the first tunnel. At the sound of her voice, they dropped from the ceiling and began to fly about, squeaking and swooping about the children's heads.

"Oh," Laura screamed, covering her hair, "Oh, *bats*—" She had both arms over her head and was huddled against Sam. "Oh, they'll get in my hair," she screamed.

"Stand still," Sam commanded. "They can't see you. They can only hear you. Don't shout like that; just stand still. I'll lead you."

He dragged the frightened girl down another passage, but it was the wrong one. There was no stone staircase like the one they had come up. "I guess we took the wrong turn," he said at last. "I think maybe we'd better go back and look for the other one."

"I'm not going near those bats again," Laura said determinedly.

Sam led the way, praying that he would come to a place that looked familiar. Now neither he nor Laura spoke. They walked on, searching each passageway for a place they knew. Finally Sam just took any passage, hoping he would stumble on the right one with luck. Laura was so frightened that she could hardly hold back the tears. Finally she said, "I don't care if the bats are back there. Let's go back and find the place we know."

But Sam was standing very still, his ears cocked to one side.

"What is it?" Laura demanded. "Do you hear something? Do you hear the others?" she asked hopefully.

Sam had been sure he had heard voices. Now he and Laura stood very still in the middle of the darkness. The candle was now extremely low and Sam searched his pocket, pulling out the last tiny stub. He lit the new candle from the old one. If only someone would see the light and come for them! But all around was deep silence. There were no voices, no sound of footsteps. Finally Sam shouted. "Here we are, *here!*"

There was no answer.

At last he and Laura turned and tried to retrace their steps. Now Laura was openly crying, no longer trying to hold back the tears. Sam himself felt close to weeping, but he put on a brave face. They crept along the inky corridor, Laura looking about fearfully for bats. They took a passage, went a short way and came up against a stone wall. Dead end! Now Sam knew that they were truly lost; he could not even find his way back to the part of the cave where the bats were.

"I never thought I'd be glad to see those bats again," Laura wailed. "But I would give anything to—Sam, we're lost, we're lost! We'll never find our way out of this awful cave. Oh, why did we ever leave the others?"

To Sam's horror, she sank to the floor of the cave and commenced to cry as if her heart would break. He tried to comfort her, but it was no use. Her sobs echoed against the walls and sounded like horrible laughter.

For a long time they remained that way, Laura on the floor crying, Sam awkwardly trying to comfort her. Finally she wiped her eyes with her hands and tried to bring up a smile. "Well," she said, "I guess there's nothing to do but keep looking."

They started out again, and this time they went more slowly, carefully exploring each section of the passageway in the hope of finding some mark that would show them the way. Sam tried shouting but at last he grew hoarse and had to give it up. The candle in his hand was dangerously low. It would only last a few more minutes. They turned into a passageway and the candle flickered, died down, and threatened to go out. "Here we are," Sam shouted in desperation, *"Here!"*

Just as the candle was about to go out, he heard an answering voice far down the passage. Sam whooped and yelled. Gradually the voices came closer just as Sam's last candle died out.

Sam never forgot that experience in the cave with Laura Hawkins. Years later he used it as the basis of one of his most exciting passages in *Tom Sawyer,* where Sam became Tom and Laura was Becky Thatcher. The boyhood experiences of Sam Clemens were to make material for much of the writing of the man Mark Twain: for the two were one and the same.

Mark Twain was born Samuel Langhorne Clemens in Florida, Missouri, on November 30, 1835. When he was four the family moved to Hannibal, a village of fifteen hundred people. The Clemens family consisted of Judge John Marshall Clemens, his wife Jane and their four children—Pamela, Orion, Sam, and Henry.

The move was the last of a long series of hopeful moves that Sam's father had made. John Clemens was originally from Virginia, one of the Southern aristocrats who had left home to seek his fortune. As a young man John Clemens had been fairly wealthy and had great promise as a lawyer. He had invested four hundred dollars—a considerable sum in those days—to buy close to a hundred thousand acres of land in Tennessee. In 1834, during a national panic, the rest of his fortune was wiped out. The Judge never seemed to overcome the bad luck that started then. He got nowhere with law. He could not do anything with his huge tract of land in Tennessee. Whatever he tried failed. But John Clemens always held on to his Tennessee land. He always believed that one day it would make the family rich.

After he lost his money, the Judge tried several ventures. He "kept store"—unsuccessfully. He rose to justice of the peace and was elected to the Surrogate Court—but misfortune still dogged him. He "went security" for a friend, Ira Stout, and Stout later declared himself bankrupt, leaving the Judge to honor the debt. Although the Judge was not legally responsible to return the money, he felt morally obligated to do so. He believed strongly in the value of a man's promise. He believed that no gentleman ever went back on his word, and he had given his word. Therefore, he would repay the money that his friend owed. Though for years his own family suffered, he religiously met the debts. But the obligations made him old before his time. He brooded on the injustice of Stout's behavior, and he thought of his own years of hardship and privation. He became silent and withdrawn—"a stern, unbending man," his son Sam wrote of him, "of splendid common sense. When he climbed upon his three-legged stool, rapped on the box which served as a desk, and demanded 'Silence in the Court,' it was fully expected silence would reign."

Sam's mother, Jane Clemens, was the last thing from solemn or dull. She was the kind of person people liked to have around, always gay, laughing, and witty. She had been a graceful dancer in her day, and she went out of her way whenever she could to take part in the town gaiety. Her life was built on laughter—laughter and affection. She was always lavishing attention on her children and her pets.

Sam's mother adored animals. Her weakness for animals was legendary in Hannibal. It was said that she scolded the cats for catching mice and that when she was forced to do away with some of the numerous kittens that the household's nineteen cats were constantly producing, she always warmed the water before she drowned the kittens.

As a young girl in Kentucky, Jane Clemens had been in love with a medical student named Barrett. There was a lover's spat and the medical student left town. Jane married the Judge to spite Barrett. The Clemens' marriage was not built on love, but the mother and father respected one another and they lived for their children. It might be hard for the Judge to show his love, but Sam's mother had no such difficulty. She went to the other extreme, forgiving her children their worst behavior, especially Sam.

Sam was her favorite. He had been born prematurely and for many months there was doubt that he would live. Jane Clemens stuffed him with "Pain-Killers"—terrible homemade medicines and local cure-alls that nearly killed first Sam and then later the cats. As soon as Sam was old enough, he secretly gave the medicine to them—when his mother wasn't looking, of course. Jane Clemens could never understand why every once in a while one of the cats went into a screaming, hollering fit.

By the time Sam was eight he was sturdy and healthy, and constantly in trouble. Getting lost in a cave with Laura Hawkins was nothing out of the ordinary for him. The dawn of each new day shone on the latest of Sammy's adventures—and misadventures.

Years later Sam sat down with his mother and asked her how she had survived his mischief. She admitted that she had been worried about him. He was always on her mind, she confessed.

"I suppose that during all that time you were uneasy about me?" Sam asked her.

"Yes, the whole time," she admitted.

"Afraid I wouldn't live?"

His mother was silent a moment, as if remembering all his boyish pranks. "No—afraid you would," she said after a pause, a twinkle in her eyes.

That was the kind of sense of humor that enlivened the family's life; the kind that Sam himself inherited from his mother.

The town of Hannibal provided the ideal background for a boy who liked to get into trouble. There were the caves a mile or so from town, where Sam and Laura had wandered away from the picnic party and gotten lost. There were cottonwood forests nearby with tempting swimming holes and abundant hunting grounds. There were boys in town who were eager to share in the excitement and adventure of hunting for buried treasure or organizing "secret" clubs. There was the endless trading of a boy's prizes to enliven the interest of their school hours. And above all there was the mighty river, the Mississippi, running right by the town.

On the river young Sam Clemens could learn the whole lore of nature. Before his eyes a fascinating world unfolded that was ten times as real as the ones he read about in his school books. He could touch and smell and see it. The school books seemed dry and dead beside the real thing. "The river," Sam said years later, "was my school."

Sam loved to swim and fish and "borrow" a boat to drift down river with the current. But he and his friends were never happier than when they were camping out on one of the islands of the broad Mississippi. There is a description of such an expedition in *Tom Sawyer*, where the feelings of young Sam are put into the words of Tom.

"When Tom awoke in the morning, he wondered where he was. He sat up and rubbed his eyes and looked around. Then he comprehended. It was the cool gray dawn, and there was a delicious sense of repose and peace in the deep pervading calm and silence of the woods. Not a leaf stirred; not a sound obtruded upon great Nature's meditation. Beaded dew-drops stood upon the leaves and grasses. A white layer of ashes covered the fire, and a thin blue breath of smoke rose straight into the air."

Young Sam Clemens had observed the marvels of nature closely. Speaking of Tom Sawyer, he says, "Now, far away in the woods a bird called; another answered; presently the hammering of a woodpecker was heard. Gradually the cool dim gray of the morning whitened, and as gradually sounds multiplied and life manifested itself. The marvel of Nature shaking off sleep and going to work unfolded itself to the musing boy. A little green worm came crawling over a dewy leaf, lifting two-thirds of his body into the air from time to time and 'sniffing around,' then proceeding again—for he was measuring, Tom said; and when the worm approached him, of its own accord, he sat as still as a stone, with his hopes rising and falling, by turns, as the creature still came toward or seemed inclined to go elsewhere; and when at last it considered a painful moment with its curved body in the air and then came decisively down upon Tom's leg and began a journey over him, his whole heart was glad—for that meant he was going to have a new suit of clothes—without the shadow of a doubt a gaudy piratical uniform . . ."

Amidst such splendor, Tom [Sam] could not contain himself. He awoke his friends and the "pirates" were soon stripped and running for the water. They fought and tumbled and chased each other, shouting and singing. "They felt no longing for the little village sleeping in the distance beyond the majestic waste of water. A vagrant current or a slight rise in the river had carried off their raft, but this only gratified them, since its going was something like burning the bridge between them and civilization." It was little wonder that Sam Clemens found school hard going when the great river beckoned him every minute.

The daily life of Hannibal went on at the same steady, slow pace as that of the river. Then, suddenly, a whistle would sound. There would be a shout, "S-t-e-a-m-boat a-comin!" and the whole town would burst into action. Within minutes men were running for the docks, boys had dropped their books or deserted their chores and were scampering for the landing, the store closed down and the owner and customers flocked down the street to see the arrival of the fabulous stern-wheeler and to gaze in silent envy at her pilot. The life of a river pilot was so glamorous that the permanent dream of every boy along the Mississippi was to take his place at the wheel of a great steamboat and be saluted as a king of the river. Young Sam Clemens of Hannibal, Missouri, dreamed the same dream as the rest.

Other exciting times in the village were the arrival of a minstrel show or a traveling mind reader. Sam himself, at the age of fourteen or fifteen, became the town hero when a hypnotist came to Hannibal with great fanfare. There were signs all over town advertising the show —twenty-five cents for adults and children half-price. The night after the first performance no one in Hannibal could talk of anything else. Sam was as enthralled as everyone else. He sat night after night in the audience trying to hypnotize himself by gazing at the hypnotist's magic disk. Grown men and women all around Sam were performing in the most outrageous way, but all the magic disk did was make him sleepy.

Finally, as he says, on the fourth night he could no longer resist temptation. After gazing at the disk for a time, he pretended to come under its spell. Then the hypnotist ran over and began waving his arms and snapping his fingers over Sam's head. The man held the disk under Sam's eyes and slowly moved away from him, leading Sam toward the center of the stage, saying that Sam must not take his eyes off the disk. Sam was as wide awake as a boy could be, but he said that "Upon suggestion I fled from snakes, passed buckets at a fire, became excited over hot steamboat races, made love to imaginary girls and kissed them, fished from the platform and landed mud cats that outweighed me—and so on, all the customary marvels."

He threw himself into the part with vigor. He was the best subject the hypnotist had ever had. All the other subjects, for instance, had failed miserably when the hypnotist asked them "what do you see?" but Sam was a miracle of inventiveness. No matter what wild notion he brought out, everyone seemed pleased.

After Sam's splendid performance, the hypnotist took no other subject, and Sam became a town legend. Night after night he went on pretending the most outlandish and foolish things. It seemed to Sam absolutely unbelievable that even the town's wisest men were taken in by his foolishness. But they all were. That lesson with the hypnotist taught him that it doesn't take much to make the wise foolish.

Beside the river entertainments, the town came to life for the Fourth of July celebration, which was the most important one of the year, more important even than Christmas. For Hannibal was on the verge of the West and patriotic sentiments were strong. There were also picnics—usually with an excursion to the notorious cave of Sam's books—camp meetings and revivals. There was skating in the winter and swimming in the summer. On the river there was an endless contest to see who could catch the biggest catfish. And of course there was school. There was no getting away from it, much as Sam tried.

There were no public schools in Hannibal, but there were two private ones, run by Mrs. Horr and Mr. Sam Cross. Pupils paid twenty-five cents a week to attend. Sam started when he was four and a half with Mrs. Horr, who taught in a small log cabin at the southern end of Main Street. Sixty-five years later, when Sam sat down to write his *Autobiography,* he still remembered his first day at school. He violated some rule and was warned that if he did so again he would be whipped. A few minutes later he was caught in the same act. Mrs. Horr told him to go out and find a switch. He looked around until he found a stick that was small, thin, and rotten. He carried that to Mrs. Horr.

The teacher then announced that she would find a boy with better judgment in selecting switches. The boy she chose, Sam says, was an expert at that sort of thing. He came in with a good thick switch that looked vicious and turned out to be twice as bad as it looked when it was applied to Sam's backsides.

Sam submitted to school—in time he even became the champion speller—but his heart was always out-of-doors. He would sit at his desk bent over a book, longing for the moment he would be free to race to the swimming hole or to go down to the pier and watch for a boat to go by. He heard the sound of birds outside the schoolroom and his mind wandered. Soon he was daydreaming over his books, his thoughts down at the levee, his lessons forgotten.

Sam's happiest times were the summers he spent on his Uncle John Quarles's farm. Here he could be with the animals, watch planting, and take part in the farm life. Uncle John's farm was four miles from Florida, Sam's birthplace, and he went to the farm for two or three of the summer months every year from the time he was four until he was eleven or twelve.

John Quarles had eight children and double that number of slaves. The farm was a big one but life went on in a relaxed manner. There was a large log house and a connecting kitchen where someone was always making a pie or cake that would tempt a boy's appetite. The farmyard was very large, fenced in on three sides by rails. There was a smoke-house for curing and storing meats, a large orchard, and a little village of Negro huts. The front yard was canopied by hickory and walnut trees, and one of the favorite autumn pastimes of the children was gathering nuts.

While Sam's family always had to scrape money together to get along, the Quarleses had plenty, and they were eager to share. The food was prodigious: fried chicken, roast pig, turkey, duck and goose; venison, squirrel, pheasant, partridge, rabbit. There were hot cakes and biscuits, homemade bread and hot rolls, hot corn pones and buckwheat cakes; and corn fresh from the garden. There were butter beans and string beans, tomatoes and peas, two kinds of white potatoes and always a big dish of sweet potatoes; buttermilk and sweet milk, clabber (milk which had thickened in souring), and watermelons, muskmelons, cantaloupes, and an assortment of pies—apple, peach, pumpkin, and berry.

In contrast to his own stern father, Sam found in Uncle John Quarles a warm humor and an easy-going manner, and he loved his Aunt Patsy's marvelous cooking and gentle touch. He loved to tease her, too, particularly by putting a harmless snake in her sewing basket. This was a trick that could be repeated over and over and always produce a first-rate reaction in his aunt who was terrified of any kind of snake.

Sam liked the slaves, too. The Quarles children were always down at the slave quarters, and Sam joined them to listen to fascinating stories and incredible superstitions. He loved to listen to the singing, and he spent hours memorizing their spirituals.

Sam had in particular one friend that he always sought out, Uncle Dan'l, "a middle-aged slave whose head was the best one in the negro quarter, whose sympathies were wide and warm and whose heart was honest and simple and knew no guile."

Sam remembered and loved Uncle Dan'l all his life, and years later when Sam wrote *The Adventures of Huckleberry Finn,* he used Uncle Dan'l's character for the Negro Jim who goes down the Mississippi with Huck.

Hannibal and the countryside around might seem sleepy and peaceful, but there was also a fierce and brutal reality that intruded on the innocence. The cruelties of slavery early came home to the boy. Sam also witnessed many feuds and fights, and he marvelled as he watched quick, deadly passions erupt into knivings and shootings.

There were frequent drownings, and year after year there was the terrible spectacle of one epidemic after another speeding through the port towns. The steamboats carried more than romance—they often were the means by which cholera and yellow fever spread up and down the Mississippi valley.

Medicines were so primitive in those days that the town paper in Hannibal recommended "soap and courage" as the treatment for cholera. Flu, scarlet fever, pneumonia, mumps—most of the illnesses that we no longer consider serious—took many lives every year, particularly among the young.

Measles was one of the most dread childhood diseases, and Sam himself nearly lost his life in the epidemic of 1845. Sam was ten then and most of his playmates were stricken. There was nearly a funeral a day. For some reason, however, Sam did not catch the disease. His mother made every effort to keep her children away from contagion. Week after week passed with the whole family waiting in fear for one of them to come down with the measles.

Finally Sam grew tired of the suspense. He decided to settle the matter in his own way. A friend, Will Bowen, lay dangerously ill, and Sam sneaked by his own mother, crept into Will's house, and got upstairs undetected. He was ready to climb into Will's bed when Will's mother discovered him and sent him home. But the second time Sam was more successful. This time he managed to get in bed with Will and remain long enough for the measles to take.

It was a serious case and everyone thought Sam was going to die. The doctor was sent for and "he put," as

Sam remembered, "hot ashes all over me. He put them on my breast, on my wrists, on my ankles; and so, very much to his astonishment—and doubtless to my regret—he dragged me back into this world and set me going again."

Doctors in Hannibal worked by the year—charging a fee of twenty-five dollars for the whole family, a good many of them furnishing medicines for the family as well. Castor oil was the main remedy, castor oil accompanied by Pain-Killers. Calomel, or camomile, rhubarb and jalap, were next in popularity. Doctors, in any case, were never called in for ordinary complaints. These were treated by the neighborhood wisdom. All the old women in town concocted their own medicines and helped dose their neighbor's children as well as their own. They would gather special herbs in the woods and compound these into formulas that had been passed along from generation to generation. It was a wonder, Sam considered later, that any of the children survived.

There were also many "faith doctors," old Indians or Negroes who had secret cures for the most common aches and ailments. In Hannibal there was an old woman outside of town whose specialty was curing the toothache. She would seize a patient, grab his jaw, peer fiercely into his face, and cry, "Believe!"

Since there were no dentists, the children preferred to let on they "believed" rather than submit to having a doctor. The doctor took his tongs and pulled out any teeth which were giving trouble, and "If the jaw remained, it was not his fault," Sam said later.

Chapter 2

Young Boy In Hannibal

Sam Clemens might be rough and ready, he might skip school and go off to make mischief on the Mississippi, he might plague his mother and tease his brothers and sister; but underneath he was also sensitive, he was alert to injustice, cruelty, suffering, sin. As a young boy he was tormented again and again by the thought that he was an "evil little boy who deserved punishment."

Sometimes when thunder and lightning seemed to be tearing Hannibal to pieces, Sam awoke and promised to turn over a new leaf. He would vow that he would not skip school, or tease Orion, or fight with Henry. He would promise God that he would try to help his mother and Pamela more and that he would obey his father at all times. But in the morning, with the sun shining, he would forget his vows and engage in some new prank. Then he would be plunged into guilt again.

Sam chafed much at the restrictions of school. As a boy on the Mississippi, growing up at a time when America was first beginning to feel its bigness and its coming greatness, he was stirred by what was happening all around him. When he was small, he saw the rush for the new territories. Every day he saw the glamorous life of the steamboat pilots. He watched pioneers passing through Hannibal on their way West. He knew the stories of the famous scouts of the frontier and the famous battles in the West. School often seemed to him a hindrance. He longed for the freedom to do what he wanted, and he wanted to do everything at once. Like most boys he could not wait to make his dreams a reality.

His restlessness got him into frequent trouble. With the side of his nature that wanted to join the pioneers or be a pilot on the river, he worshipped Tom Blankenship, the son of the town drunkard, for Tom didn't have to fuss with school, he could go barefoot when he pleased, he could swim when he wanted, he went fishing when the mood took him, he went out in a boat on the river without anyone making a fuss. Tom had no mother, and his father never cared what he did. Sam might feel sorry that Tom lacked the love of a mother and the discipline of a father, but he couldn't help envying Tom his freedom. Sam Clemens remembered and revered that happy-go-lucky boy all his life, and years later he wrote a book all about him. That book was *The Adventures of Huckleberry Finn* and the boy that Sam called Huck was really Sam's boyhood friend, Tom Blankenship.

But at the same time Sam envied Tom, he knew with another side of his nature that Tom was headed for trouble. Tom lacked discipline, he had no real knowledge, he couldn't stick to anything for any length of time. These habits might be excused in a boy but they would be blamed in a man. Already there were signs that Tom would run into difficulties when he was older.

And always before Sam's eyes was the image of his mother standing for all that was good in life. If Tom stood for the carefree, irresponsible side of life, Jane Clemens represented the well-ordered, high-principled standards of another way of living. Sam Clemens's father, it was true, also upheld this position, but the Judge did it so joylessly that it was not appealing to his young son. For Jane Clemens, however, Sam could have nothing but respect and admiration.

Sam never forgot her pluckiness. He used to say in later life that he thought his hatred of tyranny came from his mother, and he would tell the story of the time that she took on single-handed the biggest bully in town. The man was beating his daughter unmercifully, and the girl fled to the Clemens's house for help. Jane Clemens, a little woman, stood bravely in the door, the girl cowering behind her. Mrs. Clemens refused to let the angry father get near his daughter. Then she gave the bully such a talking-to that he slunk away, ashamed. Later he went around Hannibal advertising his own humiliation and calling Jane Clemens the bravest women he had ever met. Her son heartily agreed.

No, Sam Clemens could never escape the voice inside which said that skipping school was wrong, that disobeying his mother was wrong, that being willful and lazy was wrong. He was not only injuring his mother and father but he was also hurting himself. When he did wrong, he knew it. Consequently, he suffered. He felt guilty for his escapades. But he was always breaking his resolutions and getting into trouble again.

One day Sam skipped school and as it grew later and later he became more and more afraid to go home. Finally, having worried away all of the afternoon, he saw darkness come on and he thought he had better stay away. Perhaps, he thought, if he stayed away a long time, his mother and father would worry about him so much that they would forget that he had played hookey. They would be too relieved that he was safe to punish him.

He decided to hide in his father's office. He climbed in the window and went to the couch. The room was very dark and he could see nothing, but he knew the office well and he felt his way to the sofa. As he lay down, his eyes gradually made out the familiar furniture in the room. Then suddenly a cold shiver went through him. He had seen something that was not familiar at all—a figure lying on the floor!

He shut his eyes, opened them again, but the figure had not gone away. Frightened, he determined to close his eyes and count, waiting until the moonlight fell on the figure. He counted twenty, then opened his eyes. A pale patch of moonlight lay on the far side of the room.

He closed his eyes and counted to fifty. Then he lost courage and went on to a hundred. When he opened his eyes at last, a white human hand lay in the moonlight. He shut his eyes, praying, counted and looked again: an arm was now bathed in whiteness. He put his hands over his eyes and counted until he thought he had forgotten how. In the moonlight he saw the face of a man, the eyes staring straight ahead, glassy and unmoving.

The man was, indeed, dead. He had been stabbed in the breast during a quarrel in one of the local taverns. The dead man had been brought into Judge Clemens's office and had been left there until an investigation could be made. In the dim light Sam had not seen the body when he slipped through the window.

The corpse on the floor was not the only dead man to haunt his dreams. One day a tramp had passed Sam on the street. He wanted to light his pipe, but he had no matches. The tramp asked Sam for a match, and the boy gave him one. Later the tramp was arrested and put into jail. Apparently he fell alseep in jail with the lighted pipe in his hand. Perhaps he dropped the match Sam had given him on the straw-covered floor. Whatever happened, the straw covering on the floor caught fire and in a few seconds the entire cell was a mass of flames. The pitiful man screamed and pleaded for someone to save him, but there was no time. He burned to death before anyone could get to him.

Sam held himself responsible. He had given the tramp the match. The match had ignited the straw. The man had burned to death because of that match. Sam was haunted by the face of the drunken tramp pleading for someone to save him.

Now when the thunder storms shook Hannibal, Sam Clemens lay in his bed thinking that it was he the Heavens was angry with. He had been responsible for a man's death. He had come upon another man who had died violently, come upon him because he had been bad and had been trying to escape punishment.

Then came the drowning of Lem Hackett. Lem had fallen out of an empty flatboat one Sunday. The preacher, at the lesson that evening, used the boy as an example of how the evil are punished for their sins. Lem Hackett was known in Hannibal as a bad boy.

After the lesson that night Sam Clemens returned home, brooding on his own evils. There was a fearful storm that night when the "wind blew, the windows rattled, the rain swept along the roof in pelting sheets, and at the briefest of intervals the inky blackness of the night vanished, the houses over the way glared out white and blinding for a quivering instant, then the solid darkness shut down again and a splitting peal of thunder followed which seemed to rend everything in the neighborhood to shreds and splinters," Sam remembered in *Life on the Mississippi*. Sam was sure that this was Heaven's way of showing the sinful how it might punish them as it had punished Lem Hackett.

Sam was frightened half to death, sure that his own sins were being brought up for consideration. "Every time," he writes, "the lightning glared I caught my breath, and judged I was gone. In my terror and misery I meanly began to suggest other boys, and mention acts of theirs which were wickeder than mine, and peculiarly needed punishment—and I tried to pretend to myself that I was simply doing this in a casual way, and without intent to divert the heavenly attention to them for the purpose of getting rid of it myself."

Sam said it was one of the longest nights he had ever known. He endured "agonies of remorse for sins which I knew I had committed, and for others which I was not certain about, yet was sure that they had been set down against me in a book by an angel who was wiser than I and did not trust such important matters to memory."

He promised again that he would turn over a new leaf—his last—if only he were spared. All he wanted was a chance to survive so that he could prove that he meant every promise he had made.

The next morning, exhausted but thankful, Sam went out timidly, wondering who in Hannibal had been taken that night. He said he was surprised to come across a particularly well-known "sinner" on the streets, a boy whose pranks he really considered far worse than his own.

All this thunder over one small boy?

Then he had "a dim sense that perhaps the whole thing was a false alarm; that the entire turmoil had been on Lem's account and nobody else's. The world looked so bright and safe that there did not seem to be any real occasion to turn over a new leaf." Moreover, the impressive part of the argument for him was that all the other wicked boys in Hannibal were still alive.

The extraordinary thing was that three weeks later there was another drowning and another fierce and frightening storm. Only the details of the drowning this time put things in a new light—for Sam Clemens at least —on the workings of the universe.

The boy who drowned was known as "Dutchy." He was a German, a good, dull, plodding youth, who spent his time memorizing verses of the Scripture. It was said he could recite three thousand without missing a word.

Nevertheless, he got drowned, just the same as Lem

Hackett, who did not know one single line of the Bible.

Sam was a part of the events that led up to Dutchy's death. The boys were all swimming in a creek which had a sunken pile of green hickory poles. The boys would go down and see who could stay down the longest, hanging onto the poles. Dutchy was such a failure at the game that all the others made fun of him, and at last he was so angry that he begged for one last chance. This time, he said, he would stay down longer than any of the others.

Dutchy went down, but he did not come up. The boys had hidden, wanting to tease him. They thought it would be very funny if he came up and saw no one around to witness his triumph. Minute after minute passed and the German boy did not appear. The boys' laughter turned to fright. Finally they drew straws to decide who would go down and investigate. Sam lost and it was his job to go down.

Sam recalled years later that he went down and the water "was so muddy I could not see anything, but I felt around among the hoop-poles, and presently grasped a limp wrist which gave me no response—and if it had I should not have known it, I let it go with such a frightened suddenness.

"The boy had been caught among the hoop-poles and entangled there, helpless." Sam went to the surface and reported the news, but the boys were too overwhelmed by the tragedy to think of saving Dutchy. They dressed and ran away as fast as they could.

That night there was a storm worse than the one that had occurred on the night of Lem Hackett's death. The lesson for young Sam Clemens, as he tells us, was that "it convinced me that if Dutchy, with all his perfections, was not a delight, it would be vain for me to turn over a new leaf, for I must infallibly fall hopelessly short of that boy, no matter how hard I might try. Nevertheless I did turn it [his new leaf] over—a highly educated fear compelled me to do that—but succeeding days of cheerfulness and sunshine came bothering around, and within a month I had so drifted backward that again I was as lost and comfortable as ever."

There is the characteristic humor and irony in that final conclusion of Mark Twain the writer, but the truth is that Sam Clemens the boy suffered a good deal from his feelings of failure.

Sam always carried with him the picture of the tramp burning alive in the local jail. He always remembered the corpse on the floor of his father's office. He thought of the two boys that had drowned, the one such a bad boy and the other such a good one. He often dreamed of these scenes and awoke from his terrible nightmares shivering and shaking. Other times he walked in his sleep, driven by the inner torment of those events.

His troubled nights were a cause of deep concern to his mother, but Sam felt that she was so good and he was so bad that he could never explain to her his guilty conscience.

Chapter 3

Printer's Devil

S am Clemens was eleven years old when the happy round of swimming adventures, cave explorations, boating and fishing trips on the big Mississippi, school picnics and church socials, ended. In 1847 the Judge died.

Judge Clemens died just at the moment when for the first time in years the family felt fortune was about, at last, to smile on them.

All his life the Judge (like his sons later) had no head for business. His worst fault was that he was always trusting the wrong people. A rascally real estate operator let the Judge stand security for a good deal of money. For years Judge Clemens had made himself and his family practically paupers trying to make good on the money.

The year of 1847 had started, however, with high hopes. Judge Clemens was to take over the clerkship of the Circuit Court. This would mean the family was assured of a steady income. At the end of February, on a trip to Palmyra, the county-seat, where he went to be sworn in, he caught cold in a bad storm. The cold grew worse; pleurisy followed. Not even the Judge's indominable will could stop the ravages of the disease. He died on March 24th. The family finances, which had never been good, now became disastrous.

[35]

The shock on young Sam Clemens was great. He thought of his own behavior, he thought of the things his father had tried to teach him. He felt that he had failed his father, and he was filled with a grief that was intensified by his own sense of guilt.

His mother tried to reassure him, telling him that boys could not be expected to fulfill the duties of men, but Sam could not be consoled. When his mother asked him to remember the goodness of his father and try to follow that example, he hastily agreed.

Day and night he worried that he had not had the high standards his father had expected of him. He remembered all the times he had played hookey. He thought of his pranks—harmless enough, boyish pranks, but still a source of annoyance to his mother and father. He told himself that whatever else happened he would honor his father's dying request.

On his death bed Judge Clemens had told the family to "Cling to the land and wait; let nothing beguile it away from you." The land he was speaking of was the seventy thousand acres remaining of the huge tract of land in Tennessee which all his life the Judge had believed would someday make the family rich.

The land was good for nothing save potatoes, pine, and grass, but through all his troubles—starting from the time he had been wiped out in the great financial crash of 1834—the Judge had gone on thinking that the Tennessee land would be his salvation. The Judge's dream was the dream of a Virginia gentleman. In the South there was no shame in being land-poor and pride-rich; so long as there was land there was an inheritance, and the Judge had stressed this all his life to his sons. On his death bed he still spoke of it.

Even at the age of eleven Sam had doubts about the land, but Orion, the oldest son, felt as his father did. Orion was a strange boy; one of those people on whom fortune seems to frown. He was pious and somewhat priggish and he certainly was a mystery to his fun-loving mother. Jane Clemens never understood him, and later in Sam's life Orion became as much of a puzzle to him as he had been to their mother.

Orion never seemed able to hold a job, and when he did have one he always managed to lose money. In trying to explain his perplexing brother, Sam Clemens later wrote, "One of his characteristics was eagerness. He woke with an eagerness about some matter or other every morning; it consumed him all day; it perished in the night and he was on fire with a fresh new interest next morning before he could get his clothes on."

Orion was subject to tremendous shifts in interest. He would go from the heights of happiness to the depth of despair. And the shifts were sudden and unexpected. He acted on impulse, unable to settle down to thoughtful planning, always running off in a new direction after vague goals. He had no sense of proportion; everything was of equal value to him. He was the kind of person of whom we say, "He has not learned to put first things first."

Henry, the youngest boy in the family, was a gentle, good boy whose goodness was so natural that it seemed never to have occurred to him to misbehave. Henry was the model for Sid in Sam's book, *Tom Sawyer*, though Sam was to point out that "Henry was a very finer and better boy than ever Sid was."

Henry was everybody's favorite, and certainly Sam loved him like no one else in the family. But Henry could not help exasperating him. Henry was so good and he, Sam, was constantly in so much trouble!

Although the family was in desperate straits, all of them agreed not to sell the Tennessee land. Even, years later, when Sam wanted to sell, he felt a twinge of conscience. At last when he did have an opportunity to sell the land to a man who wanted to grow grapes for wine, Orion refused to sign for his share. At that time Orion had taken up a new cause. He was now a fervent teetotaler, although only a few months before he had actively campaigned against laws prohibiting drinking.

The dream of the Tennessee land never came true. Forty years after the Judge's death there were no more than ten thousand acres left, the rest having gone in small sales here and there, and no one ever made more than a couple of hundred dollars from the property. "It put our energies to sleep," Sam Clemens said in later years, "and made visionaries of us—dreamers and indolent. We were always going to be rich next year . . ."

After the Judge's death, the family was poverty-stricken. Orion went to work as a printer in St. Louis and sent as much of his wages home as possible. Pamela taught piano. Sam had a job delivering the Hannibal *Gazette*. Jane Clemens, the mother, took in boarders.

Much as Jane Clemens wanted to keep Sam in school, she couldn't. The family finances were just too bad. Sam, at twelve, became a printer's apprentice for a man named

Ament. Mr. Ament couldn't give the boy a real salary because in those days no one paid cash for newspapers. The subscriptions were paid for in sugar, coffee, wood, dry goods, pumpkins, melons, turnips, onions. The terms of Sam's contract were room and board and two suits of clothes a year.

Sam's chores included building the morning fire, getting water from the town well, sweeping out the printing establishment, sorting type, hand-setting the type and turning the press by hand. He folded and wrapped papers, and every Thursday he got up at the crack of dawn to deliver them to the town's one hundred subscribers.

Sam's mother saw how unhappy he was at the job, but there was nothing she could do. Jane Clemens was having a hard time making ends meet, and one less mouth to feed was an important consideration.

Sam's first suit of clothes were Mr. Ament's hand-me-downs, so big that they made Sam look as if he were in full sail when he came down the street. Nor did he ever see his second suit of hand-me-downs; the Aments were "forgetful" about that.

At the Aments Sam slept on the floor in the printing shop. At first he was made to eat in the kitchen, but eventually he was allowed at the dining room table. The food turned out to be a stew made mostly of potatoes, and endless boiled cabbage, one slice of bread per meal, which Mrs. Ament took the precaution of cutting (thinly) and putting at each plate. There was also watery coffee and one spoonful of brown sugar per cup, which Mrs. Ament also took the precaution of measuring out. For those who liked "white coffee," Mrs. Ament carefully measured out one teaspoon of condensed milk.

Sam was bothered day and night by hunger and felt no compunction about raiding the store room of onions and potatoes, which he and the other apprentice cooked over the stove in the printing shop.

In 1849 or 1850 Orion bought the Hannibal *Journal* on borrowed capital and good will. Orion promised Sam wages of three dollars and fifty cents a week, but there was never any money to pay him. However, when Orion was away Sam got some entertainment for himself by writing sprightly, humorous articles—mostly spoofs of local conditions and characters—and inserting them in the paper. The staid Orion disapproved of these pieces, but there was nothing he could do about them after they had already appeared.

At sixteen Sam had his first story published in a Boston weekly, the *Carpet-Bag*. It was called "The Dandy Frightening the Squatter," and it appeared under the initials S.L.C. Samuel Langhorne Clemens, alas, received no money for the piece, and had to be content with the honor, and with his hand-me-down clothes and his wageless work.

Exciting things were happening all around for the paper to report. Hannibal now possessed a telegraph machine which speeded up the flow of news from the outside world. Big events were happening everywhere. The war with Mexico ended. Then there was news of the discovery of gold in California. Nobody could talk of anything else. Then, suddenly, a new epidemic started. Cholera struck town after town. One steamboat after another unloaded its frightful cargo: passengers who had died on board. Then the word gold was heard again: the gold rush was no dream. Every day men were making fortunes out in California. Wagons flocked through Hannibal, following the old Santa Fe trail out toward Sacramento and the new wealth. Sam would stand by the wagons listening to the men talk, looking at the picks and shovels, the barrels and boxes of provisions, wishing with all his heart he could go with them. He had caught the gold fever, too.

He bemoaned his fate that he was too young to join the wagon trains. Everyone agreed there were fabulous riches to be garnered in the West. Few spoke about the suffering and tragedies that sometimes occurred. No, no one talked of Indian attacks and of deaths caused by disease, starvation, and thirst. Instead, people talked about gold, about striking it rich, about California coming into the Union.

But Sam knew he had responsibilities at home. He had to stand by and watch the men go. He talked to them and reported what he heard and sadly watched them off, wishing in his heart that he were part of the excitement and adventure.

In his few leisure hours, young Sam Clemens read everything he could get his hands on. One of the most exciting books was an account of an exploration of the Amazon. Sam thrilled to the tales of that far-off mysterious place, and he made up his mind that one day he would go to explore that other mighty river. He might not be able to go prospecting for gold in California, but he could go to the Amazon and perhaps explore the undiscovered part of the river about the headwaters. The headwaters were said to be four thousand miles from the mouth of the Amazon, and no man had ever been there—no white man at least.

But he needed money, lots of money, for such an expedition, and the Clemens household was always short of that commodity. He was not earning anything, and the paper under Orion's fretful management was not likely ever to make a fortune. Not with the kind of articles Orion liked to print! Whenever Sam could get some of his own pieces published, the subscribers all praised the writing. But Orion said it was not staid and respectable enough.

Sam read avidly about the famous World's Fair in New York. One article stated that five thousand people came every day to see the new Crystal Palace. Sam couldn't believe it. Why, that was more people by far than Hannibal had. He determined to find out what the world was like outside of Hannibal. He decided to go to New York, and after New York—the Amazon, he told himself.

At the age of eighteen Sam set out. He went by steamship to St. Louis where he worked for the *Evening News* as a typesetter, hoping to make enough money to go on to New York. Young Sam Clemens worked two months in St. Louis; then he set out for the big city with three dollars in change and a ten dollar bill in his pocket.

New York fascinated the boy who had lived in a small Mississippi river town all his life. He could not get over the elegant restaurants, the beautiful clothes, the astonishing sights. He went immediately to the Crystal Palace Fair. It cost fifty cents to enter, but it was the best half dollar Sam had ever spent. It made his head spin to see all the fabulous sights.

He went to the Croton Reservoir, at what was then the northern boundary of the city—Fifth Avenue and 42nd Street, but which is now the heart of the city and the site of the New York Public Library. He marvelled at the huge buildings with their ornate trimmings. He even saw real theater, thrilling to the great actor Edwin Forrest's performance in *The Gladiator*. But his money was quickly gone and he had to find another printing job. He worked in the city for a time, grew restless, then moved on to Philadelphia where he worked for various newspapers as a printer.

Sam was fascinated by Philadelphia just as he had been overwhelmed by New York. Here he was seeing much of American history at first hand. One after another he toured the Philadelphia museums and galleries, the libraries and historic places. He saw the grave of Benjamin Franklin and the State House where the Declaration of Independence had been signed.

He loved to go down to the harbor which linked Philadelphia to the trade routes of the Atlantic. Whenever he felt homesick for Hannibal, he would walk along the wharves of Philadelphia. As he looked down the bay, he longed to start on his exploration of the Amazon. But he was still very young and struggling along in a printing office with little hope of saving all the money he needed —at least not for years.

He probably would have stayed in the East if Orion had not ventured on a new scheme in which he needed help.

Orion had sold the Hannibal *Journal* and moved to Muscatine, Iowa. There he had started a new paper, the Muscatine *Journal*. Now he needed help and Sam answered the call, making the trip back to his brother on the train, sitting up for three days and three nights to get there.

Orion had married, and the newspaper would barely support Orion and his wife, let alone Jane Clemens, Henry, and Sam. Like Mr. Ament, Orion was paid mostly in cabbages, eggs, parsnips, cordwood, vegetables and an occasional chicken. Orion finally moved Henry and Jane Clemens to Keokuk and bought a newspaper there.

During the winter of 1856-57 in Keokuk Sam decided once and for all to make his trip to the fabulous Amazon. He knew now that Orion would never make a go of any business venture he got involved in, and Sam wanted to get out and try his own luck. The excitement and mystery of the Amazon were haunting him, and he determined that he, Sam Clemens, would be the one who would go to the headwaters and finish the exploration of one of the world's mightiest rivers.

He made his way to Cincinnati and worked until spring, carefully hoarding his money. Then, when the good weather set in, he could no longer resist the call of adventure. He was ready to take a steamboat to New Orleans and a frigate from New Orleans to South America. And then—who knew?

Chapter 4

Pilot's Cub

The Mississippi ranks with the great rivers of the world —the Amazon, Nile, Ganges, Tigris and Euphrates, Yangtze, Congo, Volga, Danube, Rio Grande, Orinoco, and St. Lawrence. Today it is *the* American river, but this claim to ownership on our part is fairly recent. The Mississippi "belonged" first to the Indians, then the French, and partially to the Spanish.

The Indians used the river extensively. Coronado, the Spanish explorer who was looking for the legendary city of gold, El Dorado, heard much about the Mississippi from Indians during his explorations in 1541. DeSoto, another Spanish adventurer who had been hunting gold in Florida, actually came upon the river as his explorations expanded westward. He is considered its discoverer, although he explored only the lower portion of the river. DeSoto himself died on its shores and his body was sunk in the Mississippi waters to prevent Indians from finding it and desecrating it.

For 132 years after DeSoto's discovery, there is no further record of white men on the river. Then in 1673 two Frenchmen, Joliet and Marquette, reached the Mississippi by way of the Great Lakes and the Wisconsin River. They were probably the first white men on the upper course of the river.

In 1682 LaSalle, another French explorer, followed the Mississippi from what is now Illinois to the river's mouth and claimed all the surrounding territory in the name of the King of France, Louis XIV. LaSalle named the area Louisiana after the King. In 1684 he returned from France to found a colony at the mouth of the Mississippi, but he was killed by one of his own men.

In 1718 Bienville founded New Orleans and extended the French North American empire from Canada to the Gulf of Mexico. Thus, in the eighteenth century the Mississippi was a French river, and the extensive lands around the river were French. In 1762, by the Treaty of Paris, the Mississippi valley east of the river—except for the site of New Orleans—was transferred from France to Spain, while the remainder of the valley was secretly ceded to Spain. Spanish control was a problem to the farmers of the then United States "West," especially Kentucky and Tennessee, and the treaty conditions for use of the Mississippi were a source of international wrangling.

The early white settlers of the Mississippi valley found the river a good way to get their merchandise from inland to the sea. Using the river was cheaper than carrying loads across the mountains. Once the products were in New Orleans they could easily be transferred by boat to the South Atlantic states, New York, or New England. To these settlers, Spanish control of both sides of the river at New Orleans was a continual annoyance.

However in 1795 Spain signed a three year treaty allowing the United States to sail their ships on the Mississippi River and to use New Orleans as a free port. At the end of the three years the Spanish governor refused to allow United States ships into New Orleans, again cutting the Mississippi River from the United States for the practical purpose of moving goods.

By 1800 Spanish rule had come to an end. Louisiana was given back to France. The settlements in the American territories, particularly those west of the Allegheny Mountains, felt strongly about closing the river. President Jefferson recognized that he had a difficult problem to deal with and that the settlers' tempers were at a dangerous pitch. Jefferson authorized Robert Livingston to try to negotiate a treaty with Napoleon for purchasing enough land to secure United States control of the Mississippi and its outlet.

Livingston went even further with Jefferson's plan. In 1803 Livingston brought off the Louisiana Purchase. At one stroke, the entire territory was annexed to America and the Mississippi became an American river.

Early traffic on the Mississippi was practically all one-way. Barges and keelboats could float down the river easily enough, but the return trip back up the river was rarely attempted. Although the voyage down went swiftly, the trip back by boat was next to impossible since the boats had to be poled by hand. A round trip could take as long as nine months.

Immigration into the Mississippi valley after the Louisiana Purchase would have been slow and difficult had it not been for the introduction of the steamboat. The steamboat was developed just a few years after the transfer of ownership of the river and its surrounding lands to the United States.

Robert Fulton, generally credited with "inventing" the steamboat, made a voyage in 1807 on the Hudson

River between New York and Albany. Fulton was not the first man to build a steamboat, but he was the first to get one running successfully in American waters. Four years after Fulton's memorable journey up the Hudson River to Albany, the first steamboat came puffing down the Mississippi.

Because of the steamboat, the Mississippi had at last become a means of quick communication and of greatly increased trade. Families who were separated could travel back and forth on visits, traveling shows could journey from town to town, and businessmen could make excursions up and down the river. New Orleans rapidly became one of the most important ports in the New World.

After 1830, the river steamer was an essential, gay, romantic part of American life, and the vessels became more and more fancy as trade became more and more lucrative. The outside of the boat was gaudy in the extreme; the inside was the last word in comfort. Each stateroom had two bunks, made up neatly and cozily. There was a closet in which to hang clothes, and a looking glass where the dandies who traveled up and down the river could admire themselves. The walls of the gilded saloons were covered with oil paintings; there were thick carpets underfoot and sparkling chandeliers overhead. On every boat there were gamblers in kid gloves, shiny boots, tall silk hats, diamond stickpins, and the latest fashion of elegantly cut English suits. Their sweethearts paraded about in feathers and finery, bows and silver buckles, loops of pearls and high hats crowned with gorgeous peacock feathers.

Meanwhile the valley itself was being populated by the kind of people who had little traffic with gamblers.

The settlers were suspicious of over-refinement and the latest styles; they believed in hard work, Christian duty, and self-denial. The Mississippi valley people were also hardy, self-reliant, and prone to judge a man by his actions, not his background. They looked askance at the "fancy" East, at the idea of first families and Mayflower descendants, and at an overcultured voice and an overstocked mind. This valley was to produce people who gave us much of the basis of our American democracy as we know it today—the pioneer creed that a man was a man when he had proved it and not because his father made money. Judge no one on family or wealth or social connections, was the cry. Judge a man on his own merit. The steamboat, with its ready access to the communities along the river, rapidly spread this spirit of the new age.

But the great period of the steamboat was to last scarcely more than fifty years. The Civil War brought an end to regular steamboat service, and after the war the Mississippi was never the same. Although many of the steamboats resumed their old routes, railroads had been greatly expanded north and south, east and west. With the coming of the railroads, the old river ports were to molder slowly away. It is impossible to overstate the contribution that the steamboat, in its brief fifty-odd years of activity, made in the development of American life. But for the coming of the steamboat, the development of the valley would probably have been postponed at least a generation, until the coming of the "iron horse."

The keelboats continued to take wares downstream for fifteen or twenty years after the advent of the steamboat. But steamers handled all the upstream business.

Keelboats carried the cargo to New Orleans and there the boats were sold and their owners returned upstream by steamboat. In Sam Clemens' youth the boys used to swim out to the floating keelboats and hitch a ride for a mile or so downstream. The keelboatmen were a rough crew, with tall yarns and rude manners, but they were basically friendly and they were usually kind to the boys.

When young Sam Clemens started off for New Orleans to get a boat to the Amazon, he saw the steamboat in all the glory of its heyday. In later years he described the sight of the boat "long and sharp and trim and pretty . . . two tall, fancy-topped chimneys, with a gilded device of some kind swung between them; a fanciful pilot house, all glass and 'gingerbread,' . . . the paddle-boxes are gorgeous with a picture or with gilded rays above the boat's name; the boiler-deck, the hurricane deck, and the texas deck are fenced and ornamented with clean white railings . . ."

Happy and excited as Sam was at the thought of his coming explorations in South America, he had not lost any of the fascination that he felt for the river pilot nor any of the awe he experienced when he heard the heady talk that went on in the pilot house. In no time at all Sam had gone up to the pilot house and made friends with Horace Bixby, who was one of the pilots on the boat he was taking to New Orleans. Soon he was spending all his waking hours chattering with the famous pilot. Bixby even let the boy steer some of the time during daylight and in the easy sections of the river.

Had Sam not been going to the Amazon, he would have liked to be a river pilot, he thought, and he confided his dreams and the excitement of his coming adventure to Bixby. He talked about the Amazon, about life on the Mississippi at Hannibal, about how he wanted to do something different and exciting from the way of life he had known.

But Sam was destined never to see the Amazon. In New Orleans he discovered there was no boat leaving for the Amazon for at least three or four years, maybe ten or twelve, some said. Others told him there was never going to be a boat.

Sam went to Horace Bixby and related this staggering disappointment. All the way down the Mississippi Sam had been bragging about how he would be afloat on the Amazon and now he had to admit his dreams were nothing but pipe dreams. Bixby listened sympathetically and then suddenly he realized what Sam was leading up to: Sam had his heart set on being a pilot *some*where. He wanted to master the Mississippi if he couldn't master the Amazon.

Finally Bixby agreed to take him as a cub on the *Paul Jones* and teach him the art of piloting for the sum of five hundred dollars. Sam had no money of his own to speak of, but he borrowed one hundred dollars from Pamela's husband and made a deal with Bixby to pay him the other four hundred when he became a licensed pilot and was earning money.

Sam had absolutely no idea what he was getting into. In the first place Bixby was not what might be called an easy teacher. He lost his patience quickly, and he had a sharp tongue. Bixby saw the ignorance of his young pilot often as stupidity and didn't hesitate to say so. But what started as abuse gradually turned to patience and understanding. Gradually Sam began, through the filter of Bixby's colorful language, to learn the tortorous windings of the Mississippi.

For it was not Bixby's temper or impatience or astonishing vocabulary that really bothered Sam, but the size of the job in front of him. When he had signed on, he had had no notion of the difficulties the job presented.

The Mississippi River is some two thousand miles long. It is also the crookedest river in the world. The river is constantly shifting; islands become peninsulas, peninsulas become islands, slight bends become in time long meanders, and these in turn become abandoned river channels with crescent-shaped lakes as the river again cuts across a peninsula.

The Mississippi can also make prodigious jumps across itself, cutting through a narrow neck of land. Often the river shortens its previous route by taking a jump of thirty miles at one time. Consequently, the distance up and down the river is continually changing. If the river were two hundred miles from one place to another and took a thirty-mile short cut, the distance would change to a hundred and seventy miles. Sometimes the cut-offs change boundaries; and in the old times, a cut-off could transfer a slave from the slave state of Missouri to the free one of Illinois, thus making a free man of him.

The river also occasionally moved sideways. At Hard Times, Louisiana, for instance, Sam Clemens later wrote that the river in his time was two miles west of its original bed. As a result, the town was no longer in Louisiana, but was now in the State of Mississippi.

In its constant flow southward the Mississippi in some places built up natural embankments or levees along the shore. These natural levees are higher than the remainder of the flood plain. Often the bed of the river actually was *higher* than the surrounding country. The natural levees were supplemented by artificial levees to protect the countryside from floods.

Sam's job was to learn every single thing that had happened, was happening or might happen on the huge river. At this time there was not one marker, not one light house, and not a single buoy or bell to help a pilot guide his boat. In addition to a total lack of navigation aids there were numerous snags, wrecks, shoals, reefs, and submerged trees that were a constant danger to steamboats. For example, a pilot would have to know the exact location of over five hundred shoal places he might meet during a trip between St. Louis and New Orleans.

When the river was very low, it was necessary to "sound" the very shallow places. Sounding was done in the following manner: The steamboat pulled into shore just before the low spot. The off-duty pilot, together with his cub and a crew of men, went out in a yawl to look for the best—that is, the deepest—water for the steamboat to pass through. The pilot on the steamboat meanwhile watched the yawl through a spyglass. He would help the men on the yawl by signalling with the boat's whistle, for the surface of the water was often easier to judge from a distance than from close at hand.

The pilot in the yawl meanwhile took the depth of the water by means of a pole ten or twelve feet long. He "sounded" the depth with the pole. Sometimes buoys were put out to mark the passage for the steamboat. The buoys were boards four or five feet long with one end turned up; at night paper lanterns with candles were fastened on top of the buoys.

Often a leadsman stood at the front of the boat to test the depth of the water. As the boat proceeded slowly along the river, the leadsman let his line out to see how deep the water was. He would call out his findings. "M-a-r-k three! M-a-r-k three! Quarter less three! Half twain! Quarter twain! M-a-r-k twain! Eight and a half! E-i-g-h-t feet! Seven and a half!" Each fathom measured six feet. The sign "Mark Twain" meant a depth of two fathoms—or twelve feet. The *Paul Jones* was a large boat and drew nine feet.

The cry of the leadsman echoed through Sam Clemens's waking mind and haunted his dreams at night. He seemed to hear inside his head over and over, "M-a-r-k seven, deep four, quarter less three, m-a-r-k twain!"

There were countless accidents on the river. Steamboats were constantly going aground, exploding, splitting in two, sinking or burning. On Hat Island alone twenty-nine boats had been lost.

Another hazard were the numerous small boats—the scows, keelboats, and rafts—that were freighting cargo down river. The steamboat had to be careful not to run them down.

Sam's first trip as a cub pilot was one that he never forgot. When the steamboat pulled away from New Orleans, Bixby began pointing out landmarks along the way. The afternoon passed pleasantly and Sam dozed and daydreamed during the first four-hour watch. During the night watch Bixby asked him what was the first point above New Orleans. Sam had to admit he could not remember.

"Don't *know?*" Bixby demanded.

Sam began to grow uneasy.

"What's the name of the *next* point?" Bixby asked. Again Sam couldn't answer.

"Well," Bixby said, disgusted, "this beats anything. Tell me the name of *any* point or place I told you."

Sam studied awhile and decided that he couldn't remember one.

Then Bixby's wrath boiled up and overflowed and "scalded" the boy. "You're the stupidest dunderhead I ever saw or ever heard of, so help me Moses!" Bixby fumed. "The idea of *you* being a pilot—*you!* Why, you don't know enough to pilot a cow down a lane. Look here! What do you suppose I told you the names of those points for?"

Sam made the mistake of telling the truth. "Well, to —to—be entertaining, I thought."

When Bixby's wrath finally subsided, he said, as if already he had given up most hope that Sam would ever make a pilot, "My boy, you must get a little memorandum-book; and every time I tell you a thing, put it down right away. There's only one way to be a pilot, and that is to get this entire river by heart. You have to know it just like A B C."

Sam eventually had a notebook that "fairly bristled with the names of towns, 'points,' bars, islands, bends, reaches, etc.; but the information was to be found only in the notebook," he writes. None of it was in his head.

Sam was in for more surprises. His first night on the boat it was forcibly driven home to him that the boat ran day *and* night. He had no sooner turned in than he felt someone rudely shaking him. "Get up," the voice said, and there was laughter from the dark.

"Ain't the new cub turned out yet?"

"He's delicate, likely. Give him some sugar in a rag and send for the chambermaid to sing 'Rock-a-by Baby' to him."

Then Bixby appeared. In a few seconds Sam was flying up to the pilot house with some of his clothes on and the rest draped over his arm.

It had never occurred to Sam Clemens that he would

Horace Bixby letting off steam

have to get up in the middle of the night and fuss with the boat. But he was on four hours, off four hours, on four hours, around the clock.

Another thing Sam discovered was that it was not enough to know the river by day. A pilot had to be able to feel his way along by night. There were no search lights for the steamboats in those days and the pilot had to depend on his knowledge of the river to guide the boat safely. This meant that the pilot had to be *absolutely* sure of where he was going. One mistake and the boat might go aground—worse, it might sink and lose a quarter of a million dollars of equipment and cargo as well as jeopardizing the lives of the passengers and crew.

Sam studied and fretted over all the observations in his notebook, and tried to memorize what he could on his off-hours.

At last he thought he had in his mind all the bends and points, islands and snags, bars and wrecks. But he was in for another shock. "My boy," said Bixby, "you've got to know the *shape* of the river perfectly. It is all there is left to steer by on a very dark night."

Sam couldn't understand how he could learn a *shape*.

"How do you follow a hall at home in the dark?" Bixby asked. "Because you know the shape of it. You can't see it." He told Sam that he would have to know the shape of the Mississippi River better than he knew the halls of his own home. Sam would have to know the river so well that he could follow the true channel regardless of how the river appeared to his eyes. At night the appearance of the river was deceptive. Bixby wanted his cub to learn to carry the shape of the river in his head, and never mind the shape before his eyes. His eyes could deceive him but he would still be able to steer by the shape in his mind.

One day when Sam was beginning to grow cocky about his knowledge, Bixby asked him if he was sure of a particular part of the river they were approaching.

"Why, I can run it with my eyes shut," Sam said confidently.

"How much water is there in it?"

Young Sam Clemens looked at Bixby. The next crossing was one of the safest on the river. The water was practically bottomless. "Why, I couldn't get bottom there with a church steeple," he said.

"You think so, do you?" Bixby said and disappeared.

There had been something in Bixby's manner which was faintly alarming, as if he had a new piece of information he wasn't telling his cub. Sam began to feel uneasy. Supposing the river had made one of its freak changes? Supposing he were to go down the usual route and run the steamboat aground? Supposing—supposing any number of things? Still he continued to steer the boat where he was sure the passage was safe.

A moment later he looked up and saw that the captain was on the hurricane deck. Shortly he was joined by a clerk, then one passenger after another. In a few moments there was a whole crowd of people staring ahead. Sam was now beyond wondering. He was sure there was something ahead that was bad, something he didn't know about.

He could not stop the boat and wait for Bixby to return. He could send a messenger after him—that would be cowardice. He stood at the wheel, filled with uneasiness.

At that instant he heard the leadsman's voice cry out "D-e-e-p four!" Deep four in a bottomless crossing! The terror of it took Sam's breath away.

The leadsman's cries began to come faster. The water was getting shallower and shallower. "M-a-r-k three! M-a-r-k three! Quarter-less-three! Half twain! Quarter twain! Quarter twain! *Mark* twain!"

All was lost. The boat was about to run aground. Sam was quaking from head to foot. He seized the speaking tube and hollered at the top of his lungs to the engineer. "Oh, Ben, if you love me, *back* her! Quick, Ben! Oh, back the immortal *soul* out of her!"

A great crescendo of sound broke in on him. It sounded to Sam like the first scraping of the boat on a reef. Then he realized what it was—laughter! Everyone was laughing at him!

The door opened quietly and Bixby stepped into the pilot house. "Didn't you know there was no bottom in that crossing," he asked.

"Yes sir, I did," Sam said.

"Very well, then. You shouldn't have allowed me or anyone else to shake your confidence in that knowledge. Try to remember that. And another thing: when you get into a dangerous place, don't turn coward. That isn't going to help matters any."

What Bixby had taught Sam was an invaluable lesson on the river or elsewhere: If you know a thing, believe in it, and don't let anyone sway you.

Chapter 5

River Tragedy

After a time Bixby decided to "farm" out his cub, and Sam was put on the *John Roe*, a slow boat known for its jolly parties and easy-going ways. Sam often sang for the company or told jokes. He was also keeping up with his reading, and he spent a good deal of his time bent over a book.

Then came his transfer to the famous steamboat *Pennsylvania*.

The *Pennsylvania* was one of the finest boats on the river and Sam could hardly believe his good fortune. He had visions of himself being the most envied cub up and down the Mississippi.

But his joy was short-lived. The pilot Sam had to work with, Tom Brown, was a miserably mean, sharply sarcastic man. He was impossible to please, incapable of understanding, and determined to making life unbearable for anyone who worked under him.

"I often wanted to kill Brown," Sam confessed in *Life on the Mississippi*, "but this would not answer. A cub had to take everything his boss gave, in the way of vigorous comment and criticism; and we all believed that there was a United States law making it a penitentiary offense to strike or threaten a pilot who was on duty.

However, I could *imagine* myself killing Brown; there was no law against that; and that was the thing I used always to do the moment I was abed. Instead of going over my river in my mind, as was my duty, I threw business aside for pleasure, and killed Brown. I killed Brown every night for months; not in old, stale, commonplace ways, but in new and picturesque ones—ways that were sometimes surprising for freshness of design and ghastliness of situation and environment."

Brown would not overlook the smallest mistake. He was always on the lookout for a fault and always finding one even if he had to invent it. Nevertheless, Sam tried to get along with him. He wanted Bixby to be proud of him and he wanted to succeed on his own.

About this time, too, his younger brother Henry wanted to go on the river. Henry had grown, at twenty, to look very much like his brother, with curly red hair and bright, sparkling eyes. Sam used his influence to get Henry a position on the *Pennsylvania* as a "mud" clerk, a position without salary. Brown ragged both the boys, but he seemed to find the gentle, good-natured Henry a special target for his criticism and complaints.

In May of 1858 things came to a head.

On that day Brown was steering and Sam was in the pilot house with him. Henry appeared on the hurricane-deck and shouted that the Captain wanted to stop a mile or so down the river. Brown said nothing, gave no sign that he had heard. But neither boy thought this was strange. Brown was such an ornery man that there was no knowing *what* he would do to spite his charges.

Sam knew that Brown was deaf (though Brown always denied this) and he thought perhaps Brown hadn't heard. He looked at the pilot and was about to say something, but knowing Brown's terrible disposition, Sam decided to keep silent. The boat went right by the plantation.

Presently the Captain appeared and demanded to know why they hadn't stopped. "Didn't Henry tell you to land here?" he asked.

"*No, sir!*" said Brown.

"I sent him up to do it."

"He *did* come up," Brown said, "And that's all the good it done, the dodderned fool. He never said anything."

Then the Captain turned to Sam. "Didn't *you* hear him?" he asked.

"Yes, sir," Sam Clemens said.

"Shut your mouth!" exploded Brown. "You never heard anything of the kind."

The Captain disappeared below deck, and the pilot ordered the boat to turn around. Sam Clemens stood in silence. About an hour later Henry came up, innocent that there had been any argument. Brown seized him immediately. "Here! Why didn't you tell me we'd got to land at that plantation."

Henry protested that he had.

"It's a lie!" Brown said furiously.

Sam could stand no more. "You lie, yourself. He did tell you," he interrupted.

Brown ordered Henry out of the pilot house and as he started out, Brown picked up a ten-pound lump of coal and started after him. Sam sprang between them.

He also snatched up a heavy stool and hit Brown so hard that Brown was stretched out.

He had committed the most unpardonable of all crimes: he had struck a pilot on duty. Sam felt that he was "booked for the penitentiary sure, and couldn't be booked any surer if I went on and squared my long account with this person while I had the chance; consequently I stuck to him and pounded him with my fists a considerable time. I do not know how long," he says, "the pleasure of it probably made it seem longer than it really was."

Meanwhile the steamboat was proceeding down river without anyone at the wheel. Presently Brown came to his senses, struggled up, and went to the wheel. Sam left the pilot house.

Of course there was the Captain to confront. He took Sam into his parlor after the watch was over, locked the door, and sat down. "So you have been fighting Mr. Brown?" he asked.

There was nothing to do but admit the truth.

"Do you know that that is a very serious matter?"

Sam had to concede that it was.

"Are you aware that this boat was plowing down the river fully five minutes with no one at the wheel?"

Sam had to admit this, too, was true.

"Did you strike him first?"

It was, again, the truth.

"With what?" the Captain asked.

"A stool, sir."

"Hard?"

"Middling, sir."

"Did it knock him down?"

"He—he fell, sir."

"Did you follow it up? Did you do anything further?"

"Yes, sir."

"What did you do?"

"Pounded him, sir."

"Pounded him?"

"Yes, sir."

"Did you pound him much? That is, severely?"

"One might call it that, sir, maybe."

"I'm deuced glad of it! Hark ye, never mention that I said that. You have been guilty of a great crime; and don't you ever be guilty of it again, on this boat. *But* —lay for him ashore! Give him a good sound thrashing, do you hear? I'll pay the expenses. Now go—and mind you, not a word of this to anybody. Clear out with you! You've been guilty of a great crime, you whelp!"

But Brown was so indignant that he insisted that Sam leave the boat. When the *Pennsylvania* reached New Orleans, the Captain gave him orders on another boat going up to St. Louis. Henry, however, was to stay behind on the *Pennsylvania.*

In New Orleans Sam often made some money by guarding the freight piles from seven at night until seven in the morning. Being paid nothing as a cub pilot, he was glad to have the chance to pick up the few dollars that the work brought him. Now he took the job again.

It was a three-night job and usually was open once a month. He was lucky to find that he could get work until his new boat left. Henry sometimes wandered down to talk with his brother around nine o'clock when his own duties were over. On the last night that Sam and Henry spent together before Henry went back to the *Pennsylvania* and Sam went to the *A. T. Lacey,* the two boys had a long talk. Sam gave Henry some advice.

They had been speaking of accidents on the steamboats and Sam said: "In case of disaster to the boat, don't lose your head—leave that unwisdom to the passengers— they are competent—they'll attend to it. But you rush for the hurricane deck, and astern to the solitary lifeboat lashed aft the wheelhouse on the port side, and obey the mate's orders—thus you will be useful. When the boat is launched, give such help as you can in getting the women and children into it, and be sure you don't try to get into it yourself. It is summer weather, the river is only a mile wide as a rule, and you can swim ashore without any trouble."

Sam did not realize how prophetic his words were to be.

A few nights later the *Pennsylvania* blew up at Ship Island, near Memphis. The great steamboat had been putting on fuel. Nearly everyone was asleep. Suddenly and unexpectedly four of the eight boilers exploded. The blast blew Henry into the river. Nothing was ever heard of Brown again.

Henry thought he was all right and remembered what his brother had told him about helping the stricken. He swam back to the boat to see what he could do for those who were hurt. In reality he was one of the worst casualties.

Sam read in one paper that Henry had been scalded, then in another that he was all right. At every port the story was different. But the truth was that he had inhaled steam and he had been scalded. When Sam finally got to his brother, he realized that there was very little hope. Day and night he sat by Henry, praying for some miracle to save his brother.

Henry was lying on a mattress on the floor with thirty or forty other patients, most of them scald and steam victims. Henry had inhaled a great quantity of steam and his body had been badly scalded. The doctors felt there was little hope. Since there were more patients than the doctors and nurses could attend, the fatally injured ones such as Henry were getting only a bare minimum of care.

But Doctor Peyton, at the urging of Sam, took over Henry's care and after a week the physician thought there was some hope of saving the boy. Finally he said Henry would get well, but that he must have a good deal of rest and quiet. If the other patients' outcries and moaning disturbed Henry, he should be given morphine, but only an eighth of a grain.

"The physicians on watch," Sam Clemens wrote many years later in his *Autobiography*, "were young fellows hardly out of the medical college and they made a mistake—they had no way of measuring the eighth of a grain of morphine, so they guessed at it and gave him a vast quantity heaped on the end of a knife blade . . ."

Henry died before light the next morning.

Chapter 6

Westward Bound

It took Sam altogether seventeen months to become a full-fledged pilot. He thought he would follow the river the rest of his life, but he reckoned without the march of events. Sam might have been forgiven for having forgotten the troublesome question of slavery while he basked in the glory of being a river pilot. For he was only twenty-five years old, he was making two hundred and fifty dollars a month, and he was popular and sought after wherever he went.

He had taken to writing again, too. He was still interested in humorous sketches that poked fun at some of the high and mighty airs of the people he knew and at himself as well. But he did not sign the initials S.L.C. to one of his latest pieces. There was a Captain Isaiah Sellers who wrote highly-respected but long-winded articles about navigating conditions on the Mississippi. Captain Sellers was in his sixties, and was considered an authority on the river. But he had a habit of being overly solemn in his writing and terribly round about at getting to the point.

Sam Clemens decided to write a spoof of Captain Sellers. At one point the Captain had adopted the pen name of Mark Twain, and when Sam did his take-off on Sellers, he used the same signature. The old man was terribly hurt at being made fun of. Sam had not meant to hurt him because he respected Captain Seller's knowledge and his position. Sam promised himself that he would never use the name of Mark Twain again.

Popular, happy Sam Clemens thought he hadn't a worry in the world save having hurt the old Captain. But he had forgotten that others did. The problem of slavery was one no man in the United States could ignore.

The year 1860, it turned out, was the end of an era, the end of the steamboat era on the Mississippi, and the end of a whole way of life for the South.

In November of 1860 Abraham Lincoln was elected President. South Carolina left the Union. By February of 1861, South Carolina had been joined by seven more states who proclaimed themselves the Confederated States of America. Early on the morning of April 12, 1861, troops of South Carolina fired on Fort Sumter, a Federal fort in the harbor of Charleston. Three days afterwards war started; President Lincoln sent out the call for volunteers to uphold one nation indivisible, with liberty and justice *for all.*

Almost immediately river traffic was disrupted. The Mississippi itself knew no difference between north and south; but the pilots did. They were bewildered and disbelieving. Many pilots deserted the river and joined the Federalists or the Confederates. Horace Bixby went with the Union forces, as a pilot on the Missouri River.

Soon trouble began. Boats were fired on.

Sam Clemens had been born in the South and he had been raised with people who regarded slavery as normal. He knew that slaves were frequently separated from their families and that they lived a hard life of toil. As a young boy he had seen an act of brutality by a slaveowner that had sickened him.

But all around him people had said that slavery was right. The Missouri newspapers he worked for often defended it, preachers defended it, and his friends defended it. Some members of the Clemens family were individualists, however. Long before Sam himself came to see the terrible evils and destructive forces of a system which permitted one man to own another and use him any way he wanted, Sam's older brother Orion came out for the abolition of slavery. An abolitionist, as Orion called himself, was looked on in Hannibal as worse than a horse thief, but Orion stuck to his principles.

Hannibal's slavery was of the household, domestic kind, not the fierce tyranny of some of the cotton or tobacco plantations. The Negro families were rarely separated, and then only in cases where the white master had no choice. Nevertheless, slaves were sometimes "sold down the river" to work on plantations in the Deep South and the scene as the man or woman departed was a painful one to watch. It was terrible for a husband or wife to know that he or she would be parted from the family. It was still worse to think that that family would never be reunited, that children often grew up without knowing their mother or father, and that husbands and wives were separated forever.

All his life Sam Clemens remembered a little colored boy, Sandy, who sang constantly, hour after hour, a steady droning. One day Sam lost his temper and went to his mother, complaining that he could no longer bear Sandy's incessant singing.

Jane Clemens looked at her son and said, "When he

sings it shows that he is not remembering and that comforts me; but when he is still I am afraid he is thinking and I cannot bear it. He will never see his mother again; if he can sing I must not hinder it, but be thankful for it. If you were older you would understand me; then that friendless child's noise would make you glad."

When Sam was older, he did remember, and understand, and he thought of the singing then as his mother had: with gladness that the child had for that moment forgotten his grief.

The Clemenses were poor and rarely had more than one slave to help out. For years they had a girl, Jennie, but in the end she had to be sold down river. The family's finances made the sale necessary and the girl herself asked to be sold, thinking she would better her lot. But Sam was troubled by her departure. He wondered what awaited Jennie down the river and was convinced whatever it was, it would be far worse than life in Hannibal.

Then, too, Sam had once seen a runaway slave from Florida with his white captors. He remembered how the white men had tied the slave and left him in a deserted shack. The slave had suffered fearfully, lying on the ground crying and pleading for mercy. Another time Sam had seen a man hit his slave with a piece of iron slag. The slave had died. But a slave was only a piece of property, no more; the man had not mourned for the dead man but for the loss of a valuable piece of property. Sam Clemens could not forget that death. It bothered him for years.

Only on the Quarles farm had Sam found consolation. There the color of a man's skin seemed to have no real significance. True, Uncle John Quarles and Aunt Patsy owned slaves, but each one had some importance. Each seemed to be a unique part of the household. But later in his life, when he was writing his *Autobiography,* Sam realized that "We were comrades and yet not comrades; color and condition interposed a subtle line which both parties were conscious of and which rendered complete fusion impossible."

He also remarked that "In my schoolboy days I had no aversion to slavery. I was not aware that there was anything wrong about it. No one arraigned it in my hearing; the local papers said nothing against it; the local pulpit taught us that God approved it, that it was a holy thing and that the doubter need only look in the Bible if he wished to settle his mind . . . In Hannibal we seldom saw a slave misused, on the [Quarles] farm never."

But in 1860, there was no longer any question that the slavery issue was the most important one in the nation. Arguments went on every hour—hot, impassioned arguments that sometimes led to fights. Speeches, editorials, debates were in the newspapers every day.

The Northern members of Congress had pushed through laws which put high tariffs on imports. These tariffs greatly raised the price of goods which Southerners imported from Europe. In return, the Southerners managed to get the Fugitive Slave Law passed. This law gave a slave owner the right to repossess slaves who had escaped to the North in search of freedom. The Fugitive Slave Law brought to a head all the bad feeling that had been building up on both sides.

There was no question that many of the abolitionists (people who wanted the slaves freed) were fanatics —men who had lost all sight of reason in their devotion to their ideals. But the South had its fanatics, too. There were Southerners who had said that if they could not keep their slaves and bring them back when they ran away, they would leave the Union. Now, at last, they had put that threat into action.

It was a time of hard decisions. Many men of level head in other things completely lost their senses when the question of slavery arose. Tempers became hot, families took opposite sides and argued and quarreled and sometimes retreated into bitter silence. But there was no question, as Abraham Lincoln had proclaimed, that "this government cannot endure permanently half slave and half free."

Because the war had completely disrupted travel on the Mississippi, Sam's river days were over. He had eight hundred dollars, in silver, when he started back toward Hannibal. He was weighed down with money and with doubt about what he should do. Finally he decided to join a friend who had gotten together a group of militia to serve with the Confederacy.

The boys were disorganized, unfamiliar with weapons, and—if the truth were known—jumpy and jittery. Sam soon recognized that he hadn't the stomach for serious fighting, but he stayed with the group until an incident occurred which determined him never again to point a gun at a man if he could possibly avoid it.

The ragged little band of militia had been on one maneuver after another, afraid of an enemy which apparently had no interest in them. The boys thought they saw Yankees in every tree and shrub, and they continually retreated before an army which did not exist. One night, at a corncrib that was their headquarters, they were all asleep when they heard the sound of someone on horseback close by. Alarmed, the cry went up that it was a Yank. Someone fired; then there was another shot. In the end six rounds were fired and the horseman fell dead.

It was not a Yank soldier but some stranger. Sam Clemens had fired one of the shots, and he held himself personally responsible for the man's death. So far as he was concerned, this was the end of his fighting. The random killing of a stranger who had done neither Sam nor the other boys any harm was as meaningless as anything could be. Three weeks in the militia had been enough to teach Sam the worst of all lessons of war: the man we shoot is flesh-and-blood like ourselves. He resigned from the Confederacy and went home.

A senseless, stupid killing

[73]

The gold rush of '49 and its excited, adventurous prospectors had never left Sam's mind. Now news of a new strike—this time in silver—renewed all the furor and excitement of the years before. It was reported that in Nevada there were silver deposits beyond the riches of California's gold. Men were pouring into the region with all the hope and expectation of the California forty-niners.

Even Orion, staid, placid, respectable Orion, had the fever.

Orion was going to be Secretary of the new Territory of Nevada. He was to be paid eighteen hundred dollars a year and to have an office in Carson City, the capital of the Territory. And even better, Orion wanted Sam to accompany him as his own private secretary.

There was only one hitch: although Orion was all ready to start his new career, he had no money. Sam did not hesitate to offer to pay Orion's fare. Sam's imagination was already fired with the idea of prospecting, and he couldn't wait to get on his way. He still had money saved up from his days as a pilot on the Mississippi, and in August, 1861, he and Orion started out for the new territory of Nevada, taking a steamboat up the Missouri River. The trip took six days and the river seemed to Sam paltry and uninteresting in comparison with the mighty Mississippi.

At St. Joseph, Missouri, Orion and Sam took the Overland Stage. The fare was one hundred and fifty dollars apiece, which Sam paid. There were no railroads west of Chicago, so there was either the choice of going overland by stagecoach or going by boat to Panama and then overland to the Pacific and from there by boat to some place near their destination. Orion and Sam preferred the stage journey to the long sea trip.

The baggage allowance on the coach was twenty-five pounds per passenger, and the two brothers had to leave behind a good deal of their stuff. Orion insisted on keeping his Unabridged Dictionary, a big, unwieldy book that was to cause no end of trouble.

The stage left at eight o'clock in the morning, and the horses sprang out into a summer morning brilliant with sunshine. The coach was drawn by horses that were especially developed for their speed and strength. The coach itself could carry from eight to fourteen passengers, their baggage, and its most important cargo—the overland mail. Two passengers rode up front with the driver, and the rest rode inside. To help reduce the jolting, the coach was supported by two leather straps called "thorough braces."

The trip from St. Joseph, Missouri, to Sacramento, California, was nineteen hundred miles and a stagecoach usually made it in fifteen days. The mail contracts said that the trip should be made in eighteen or nineteen days which made allowance for bad storms, winter snows, and breakdowns. For each two hundred and fifty miles of territory there was an agent, and his area was called a division.

The agent bought provisions for men and horses, purchased mules, harnesses, and horses, and was in charge of the stage coach stations. The agent was also supposed to maintain order and discipline—frequently his hardest job. There were eight or ten of these "kings" along the stagecoach route, and they were equal in arrogance and importance to the old river pilots.

Next in rank, says Sam Clemens, came the division agent's conductor. "His beat was the same length as the agent's—two hundred and fifty miles. He sat with the driver, and (when necessary) rode that fearful distance, night and day, without other rest or sleep than what he could get perched thus on top of the flying vehicle.

"He had absolute charge of the mails, express matter, passengers, and stage-coach, until he delivered them to the next conductor, and got his receipt for them."

In all there were close to eighteen conductors, more conductors than agents, because stages traveled both ways, and there had to be a conductor for each stage.

After the conductor, in order of importance, came the driver. His hours were long and his time to sleep short. At regular intervals the stage got a new driver, and theoretically each driver had ample opportunity to rest up. But occasionally a driver got sick or the coach ran into trouble, and so the old coach driver had to continue on for many extra hours. If the trail was smooth, the driver would sometimes snatch twenty or thirty minutes of sleep; instinct told him to hold on when there was a sharp jolt or bump.

Soon Orion and Sam were in Kansas, a land of rolling plains covered with corn fields, like a sea of tassles and spears running a hundred miles away to the horizon. Their coach had six handsome horses, but there were only three passengers, the remainder of the coach being full of mail bags. The coach was carrying three days' delayed mails, twenty-seven hundred pounds of it. Horses were changed every ten miles throughout the day, and the fresh horses kept up a fast speed.

One night the leather belt that went through the

braces and supported the coach suddenly snapped. The exhausted passengers piled out and slept on the roadside until the break was repaired. But when they got back in again, Sam found that the thoughtful coach driver had piled the mail between the seats. They had beds—real if somewhat lumpy beds—that night.

After the thorough brace broke, the driver abandoned some of the mail, but Orion still hung on to the Unabridged Dictionary.

The most interesting part of the long, dusty trip for Sam and Orion was their arrival at one of the stations. First the stage coach driver blew his horn to announce the stage's arrival. The horses seem to sense that they were near water and rest, and the stagecoach leapt ahead and clattered to the door of the station house. There were shouts of welcome from inside, and shouts of thanksgiving from the weary passengers. But Sam soon learned that all attention was focused on the stagecoach driver. Like the river pilot, he was a prince among men, envied and admired beyond all expectation.

The station stops were all adobe—a cluster of low, sun-dried, mud-colored buildings which made a picturesque silhouette against the sky. The roofs were flat, made of thatch and then sodded or covered with earth. Often weeds sprang up from the mud-covered roofs of the station, the barn, the stable room for the horses, and the hut which served as an eating place for the passengers. Back of the eating room was a small partitioned cubicle with a couple of bunks for the station keeper and a visitor or two. There were no windows as such, only square holes to let in air and certainly big enough for all the bugs in the vicinity.

A fireplace served for warmth and cooking. In a corner of the eating room stood a sack of flour, some tin coffee pots, a bag of salt, and usually a side of bacon. There was water for washing, but the stage passengers were expected to carry their own soap and towels.

The station men were rough characters—frequently outlaws from the Eastern states. They dressed in coarse woven pantaloons patched with buckskin, and with the ends of the pants stuffed into high boots. The boots had high heels and were armed with spurs. Most of the desperados wore beards—probably either from laziness or as a disguise—and their uncombed hair was covered by an old slouch hat. All the men carried revolvers and bowie knives, the latter tucked into the tops of their great boots.

A battered tin plate with a knife and fork and a tin cup were placed on a greasy table for a passenger to eat from. The food almost invariably consisted of stale bread, a slice of bacon (usually condemned, uneatable army bacon from a nearby fort), and a concoction called "slumgullion," which was supposed to be tea. There was no milk or sugar, not even a spoon to stir the slumgullion with. Coffee was an unheard of luxury.

After three hundred miles, Sam caught sight of the Platte River, and suddenly the prairies came to life. Coyotes ran alongside the stage coach. He saw antelope, and sometimes a wolf. The scenery itself, however, remained for the most part flat and monotonous.

But the stage in which Sam and Orion left St. Joseph was not scheduled to make the whole trip to Carson City. At Julesburg, Colorado, Sam and his brother transferred to a smaller coach called a mud wagon, which was said to be strong enough to get through the creek beds and over the mountain ridges farther West.

Alas, not far out of Julesburg the mud wagon broke down. While it was being repaired, Sam took the opportunity to go buffalo hunting. But the hunt "ended in disaster and disgrace, for a wounded buffalo bull chased the passenger Bemis nearly two miles, and then he [Bemis] forsook his horse and took to a lone tree."

When the mud wagon was on its way again, the passengers settled down to fatigue, boredom, and a tremendous amount of bouncing. Mile after mile of plains fled by the stage window, the monotony relieved every once in a while by a huge jack rabbit that made off for the horizon.

Since there were no ladies at the stations or in the stagecoach, the men stripped to their underclothing early in the morning to combat the terrible heat of the day. They were always careful, however, to make sure that their pistols were within easy reach. At night they kept the guns where they could put their hands on them at once. Orion's Unabridged Dictionary was never still for long in the bouncing mud wagon. It had a way of banging a sleeping person on the head or landing with a thud on someone who had taken to daydreaming over the monotonous landscape.

One time the driver let out a shout. All the passengers craned their necks to see what was the matter, fearing that the shout might signal unfriendly Indians. In the far distance Sam saw a lonely rider making his way at unbelievable speed across the landscape. The Pony Express!

The Pony Express service took mail between St. Joseph, Missouri, and Sacramento, California, covering the same distance as the stagecoaches, nineteen hundred miles. The riders rode day and night at breakneck speed, but the trip still took eight days.

The Pony Express rider went fifty miles without stopping "by daylight, moonlight, star light, or through the blackness of darkness." Although the horses were fine racing creatures, they could not keep up the speed for more than ten miles, and the rider changed mounts at a station where two men held a fresh horse. The rider and horse traveled "light:" the rider, for that matter, traveled so light that he did not carry arms. The horse had a small racing-type saddle, no blanket, lightweight shoes or none at all, and the small mail packet was strapped to the rider's thighs and was the size of a small, thin book.

In order to make all speed possible, the company had eighty riders and four hundred horses. The service was in reality one long race—a race against unseen opponents, a race against time, exhaustion, Indians, weather, and fatigue.

The Pony Express had been established by the U. S. government when a crisis of the impending Civil War made news between the U. S. and California necessary. It only lasted eighteen months, but the picturesqueness and bravery of the men made it a part of Western lore.

As the rider passed the mud wagon, the passengers gave him a cheer. He looked up for a brief moment, smiled, waved, and was past almost at the same instant. A few minutes later he had disappeared in a cloud of dust.

Chapter 7

Carson City and the Comstock

Fort Laramie! The wagon passed through at night and the passengers found themselves in the Black Hills. That was the beginning of real danger from the Indians. Sam was told that at all costs the passengers should keep their windows curtained, and at night he and Orion sat up, guns ready for trouble.

The night before one of the Pony Express riders had been shot and wounded by an Indian. All the men were uneasy and kept their guns at hand. At last Sam Clemens fell asleep. He was troubled by dreams of hostile Indians and ambushes as he tossed and turned, avoiding the Unabridged Dictionary.

There was danger not only from hostile Indians but also from desperados lurking in the mountains. The men in this region were a fierce breed, many of them in trouble with the law and hiding out at the little-known stopping stations. Criminals who were wanted for murder, thievery and extortion often became station attendants, and it was not unusual for the men who congregated there to drink, play cards, and get into bitter arguments.

There had been so much trouble at these stations outside Fort Laramie that the company had finally hired a man to keep order. His method, though drastic, produced results. He stopped the fighting and kept the peace by hanging or shooting anyone who disobeyed his orders. Slade was the man's name and he was known as one of the most ruthless of a breed of ruthless men, a man whom even the most dangerous outlaw respected.

Slade was a division agent who would stop at nothing to have his own way. "A high and efficient servant of the Overland, an outlaw among outlaws and yet their relentless scourge, Slade was at once the most bloody, the most dangerous, and the most valuable citizen that inhabited the savage fastnesses of the mountains," Sam Clemens wrote of him.

Slade had been born in Illinois of a good family. When he was in his middle twenties he killed a man and had to leave the state. He had gone West and joined one of the wagon trains. One day he and another of the wagon drivers had had a bitter argument. The two men had drawn but the other man had been quicker. Slade said quickly that wasting life over so trivial a slight was silly and that it would be better for the two of them to fight it out with their fists. The other drive threw down his pistol, whereupon Slade shot him dead.

An Illinois sheriff was hunting Slade, and he would have to answer to the other men of the wagon train if they caught up with him. So Slade kept moving, fighting Indians, and gaining a name for himself as a merciless fighter.

It was this reputation that finally brought him the job of Overland division agent first at Julesburg. The post at Julesburg, when he got there, had been the one most plagued by troubles—stolen horses, delayed coaches, outlaw raids, and missing supplies. Slade made short shrift of the problems. He had to kill several men to get his coaches through on time, but now there was not a coach on that line that was off schedule.

After Slade cleaned up Julesburg, he was transferred to the Rocky Ridge division of the route. This, says Sam Clemens, was "the very paradise of outlaws and desperados. There was absolutely no semblance of law there. Violence was the rule. Force was the only recognized authority. The commonest misunderstandings were settled on the spot with the revolver or the knife."

Slade was in his element. He raided the outlaws, recovered stolen stock and a number of purloined horses, killed those desperados who would not fall in line and forced the rest out of the district. He captured two men who had stolen Overland property and hanged them himself as an example to others. He was jury and judge alike, a matchless marksman, and a man seemingly incapable of fear. It was said that Slade had learned from the Indians to cut off the ears of his victims and to keep them as mementoes or to send them to those who would best learn by the gruesome warning.

All along the route Sam and the passengers heard one terrible tale after another about Slade.

In due time excitement died away and the passengers became numbed by the monotony of the landscape. The Unabridged Dictionary kept things lively now and then, but for the most part the trip was one of dull indifference on the part of the passengers, punctuated by stops at the stations for cups of slumgullion and crusts of dried bread.

At one of the stage stations the group sat down to breakfast among a particularly savage-looking group of men. Sam, wanting to disassociate himself from trouble even before it began, seated himself on the other side of the room next to a quiet, gentlemanly-looking man who was sipping from a tin cup. Sam was congratulating himself on the cup of coffee that he had been fortunate to get when suddenly in the middle of his coffee Sam heard someone address his companion as *Slade!*

Sam sat as one paralyzed. The coffee in his cup was gone, but he made no move to get more. Then the supply of coffee ran low; there was only one cupful left, and Slade reached over to take that when his eyes fell on Sam's empty cup.

Slade tried to press the last of the coffee on Sam and Sam just as politely kept declining. He was, he said, afraid that Slade "had not killed anybody that morning, and might be needing diversion."

Slade insisted that he take the last cup and Sam finally did, but he drank it without enjoyment, for he "could not feel sure he [Slade] would not be sorry, presently, that he had given it away, and proceed to kill me to distract his thoughts from his loss."

Gradually the mud wagon went into the hills; the scenery was breath-taking now; the heat gave way to coolness, there were big trees and clear, high skies.

The wagon passed a Mormon emigrant train of thirty-three wagons. At Horse Creek the passengers had an unheard of luxury, a bath. It was not a real bath, of course, but the driver stopped long enough for them to wash themselves in a mountain stream.

There was a change of mules ten or twelve times each day and Sam was astounded to see that the entire process took only four minutes. Six fresh mules, all harnessed, were waiting at each station. The old ones were out and the new ones in in the time it took to exchange greetings with the station master.

The wagon continued on, leaving the Wind River and Uinta Mountains behind, and passed through land of fabulous scenery, though the view was often marred by "long ranks of white skeletons of mules and often—monuments of the huge emigration of other days —and here and there were up-ended boards or small piles of stones which the driver said marked the resting-place of more precious remains."

Sam ate his first decent food since the beginning of the trip at the Green River station—hot biscuits, fresh antelope steaks, and good hot coffee. Then the wagon went on, stopping over in Salt Lake City, where Sam was curious about the Mormons and spent some time visiting the famous sights and questioning many people about the beliefs of the sect and its leader, Brigham Young. In Salt Lake City Orion and Sam stocked up with enough bread, boiled ham, and hard-boiled eggs to last the rest of the six hundred miles that lay ahead, and thereby freed themselves from the tyranny of slumgullion and stale bread.

Sam and Orion had been traveling for days. It seemed to them that they would never be able to sit up straight again. Then suddenly in the distance they glimpsed their destination: Carson City, the Capital of the Territory of Nevada, named after the famous scout and hunter Christopher—Kit—Carson.

It would be hard to imagine a place more disappointing. The town was nothing but rough wooden

Carson City, Nevada—land of prospectors, pistols, pioneers

houses tacked together and stores without much to sell, a tiny congestion of flimsy buildings in the midst of the great Nevada landscape. The capital of the Territory was a sad-looking spectacle where two thousand people lived in catch-as-catch-can houses. The main street had only four or five squares of one-story wooden stores, fronted with board sidewalks that rattled when walked upon. The town boasted a "plaza," a large, unfenced vacant lot with a liberty pole in the middle, but which seldom saw anyone promenading on it. It was used for public auctions, for community meetings, and as a place to swap horses. Teamsters frequently camped there. It was about as elegant as a littered alleyway back "East."

But Carson City was the hub of the mining craze. Day and night miners galloped into town with the reports of the latest finds. There were ranchers from the surrounding territory, and passing travelers were frequently riding in. All these men seemed quick to lose their tempers and fast to use their guns. Scarcely a day passed without a gun duel of one sort or another. A hot, dry wind blew dust over everything; the whole town was covered with a patina of white, fine dust from the "Washoe Zephyr," Washoe being the nickname for Nevada.

The governor's house was distinguished by the fact that it had two rooms. Governor Nye was to have a legislature composed of miners. The work was erratic; the pay only three dollars a day when room and board often ran four or four and a half—but many men were anxious to serve out of patriotism. Carson City had only been a capital since 1861, six months before Orion's appointment. The territory was part of the land ceded to the United States after the Mexican War. At first the territory had been a part of the Utah territory, but after silver was discovered, Nevada was made a separate territory. The recklessness and lawlessness of the miners who had gone out to the new territory was well-known. Now there was to be law and order. Lincoln had appointed Governor Nye to set it up.

The legislative hall was something of a shock: a small, rough room divided by a canvas partition—one side for the House of Representatives, the other for the Senate.

The canvas partition had been Orion's inspiration; originally the stone building, which a private citizen had donated, had been one large room. Orion paid $3.40 for the canvas, but the U. S. Government refused to honor his voucher, claiming that the sum was an extravagance. Orion ended up paying for the partition out of his own pocket.

The legislative session was a sixty-day meeting in which fighting took up as much time as law-making.

Sam quickly adopted the garb of the town—a slouch hat, blue woolen shirt, and pants jammed into his boots, and he felt himself a real Westerner. Presently he heard of the incredible beauty of a lake nearby, the now-famous Lake Tahoe, and curiosity finally made him take a camping trip out to see its splendors. He camped and fished, and fell in love with the lake.

On his return to Carson City he was determined to buy a horse, even though he knew nothing about them. But all Westerners worth the name had horses. Very well, he would have a horse.

He was sold a "Genuine Mexican Plug," and thought he was fortunate to get such a splendid animal for only twenty-seven dollars. The horse had one thing that could be counted in his favor: it bucked whenever given the chance. The first time Sam mounted, he was quickly bounced out of the saddle.

It was not long until the truth came out. "Stranger," said an elderly man, "You've been taken in. Everybody in this camp knows that horse. Any child, any Injun, could have told you that he'd buck; he is the worst devil to buck on the continent of America.

"And moreover," the old man continued, "he is a simon-pure, out-and-out, genuine d——d Mexican plug, and an uncommon mean one at that, too. Why, you turnip, if you had laid low and kept dark, there's chances to buy an *American* horse for mighty little more than you paid for that bloody old foreign relic."

Sam could not auction the plug off. He could not sell him. He could not even give the animal away. There seemed no way of getting rid of the Genuine Mexican Plug. At last he managed to pass the plug off on an Arkansas traveler who was passing through.

Orion fell into his government job with gusto, but Sam, Orion's unpaid secretary, was restless. He wanted to go prospecting and make his fortune as everyone else was doing. Fortunes were being made right and left. Every day there were new stories of strikes, of penniless miners who were now worth a fortune. The town loafer had gone to sleep one night and had awakened the next morning to find himself worth a hundred thousand dollars. Esmeralda had come in and people said Humboldt was next.

Chapter *8*

Searching for Silver

What gold had been to California, silver was now to Nevada. And Sam Clemens was itching to try his luck prospecting. It would have been a strange young man indeed who was not excited by the stories of the enormous fortunes that were being made on every side.

The word *Humboldt* was on everyone's lips. People were saying that the Humboldt strike would prove greater than the famous Comstock Lode, the rich silver vein which had been discovered near Virginia City in 1857 and which had started thousands of miners on a new migration.

A little over six weeks after Orion and Sam arrived, there was another big strike, and Sam saw this as the opportunity to make his fortune: rumor said that for every hundred pounds of ore that came from the Humboldt Mountain there was two or three times as much silver as in Comstock ore.

Sam and two friends, Billy Clagget and A. W. Oliver, both young lawyers, decided to go prospecting together. They selected as a guide a young blacksmith, Ballou, who actually had had some experience mining and who also recommended himself as a cook. The four started off with the usual equipment for mining: a couple of horses and a wagon loaded down with tools, pickaxes, supplies, and "snake medicine." On this trip there was also a cribbage board and a book of hymns. Orion kept the Unabridged Dictionary in Carson City.

The trip to the Humboldt region was difficult in the extreme. There was no marked road to follow, and the horses had a hard time making their way with the heavy load. Often the party bogged down in sand and the four men had to get out and push and heave until they managed to free the horses and cart. The amount of provisions, the rough terrain, and the problems with the horses soon wore them out.

"The horses dragged the wagon two miles from town and then gave out," Sam Clemens reminisced in *Innocents Abroad,* recalling that terrible time, "pushing through sand that had no bottom; toiling all day long by the wrecks of a thousand wagons, the skeletons of ten thousand oxen; by wagon-tires enough to hoop the Washington Monument to the top, and ox-chains enough to girdle Long Island; by human graves; with our throats parched always with thirst; lips bleeding from the alkali dust; hungry, perspiring, and very, very weary—so weary that when we dropped in the sand every fifty yards to rest the horses, we could hardly keep from going to sleep . . ."

To add to their difficulties, they ran into trouble with Indians. For a moment Sam thought he had seen his last day on earth, but the Indians turned out to be more interested in presents than scalps. The party was allowed to continue after giving the Indians some gifts.

The party went on, bouyed by the hope of making their fortune. What, they asked themselves, was a little hardship in the face of a lifetime of wealth? But when they at last reached the mining settlement, they saw that conditions there were possibly even worse than those they had experienced on the trail.

It had taken fifteen days to make the trip of two hundred miles, thirteen really, for they had stopped once for a couple of days to allow the horses to regain their strength. The four arrived in Unionville, Humboldt County, through a blinding snow storm. If Carson City had been something of a disappointment to Sam, Unionville was more so. The whole "town" consisted of eleven cabins and the everpresent liberty pole.

The men got to work constructing the typical "Humboldt house." They dug a square in the steep side of the mountain and then set up two uprights which they topped with two joists. Over these they stretched a sheet of home-made cotton cloth forming a roof; the sides and back were dirt walls which the digging had provided. They made a chimney simply by turning back a flap of the corner of the roof.

Ballou was the most experienced miner of the four, which wasn't saying much, and he was elected to direct operations. Sam had had the notion that they could wander around the mountainsides picking up nuggets as big as their fists, and that their fortunes would be made in a matter of days. He turned out to be mistaken.

Ballou set the group to digging in the snow-covered mountainside, a back-breaking chore. The four men pitched in and worked as hard as they could, but they didn't discover any silver. One day Ballou reported he thought he had found a good place. The four began digging, and they made excavations in the rock. They planned to blast with dynamite. But Ballou decided that to find anything worthwhile they needed to sink a shaft. They simply had not the tools for such an extensive operation. Although they sent a claim to the mining office, hoping to sell their find, no one seemed interested. One disappointment followed another, and their resources were running low. Sam began to think the mining business made more paupers than princes.

Orion and Sam had bought feet in various of the Esmeralda mines, and Sam thought that he might do well to go over there to check how their investments were making out. He set out with Ballou and a Prussian, Ollendorff, but the two lawyers said that they had had enough mining. They would stay in Humboldt and practice law. The miners were always having squabbles and the two men thought they might make their fortunes out of quarrels instead of silver.

Ballou, Sam, and Ollendorff started off with high hopes. It seemed to Sam that leaving Humboldt was one of the wisest decisions he had ever made, but he had not gone very far when he wondered if bad luck were not stalking him.

A few hours after their departure, the three men found themselves in the midst of a bad snow storm. They were determined to go on, but the storm grew worse and worse. The three agreed that they had to keep moving or they would freeze. The horses stumbled and refused to get up; Ballou swore at them and pulled and tugged, but each time they went down he had a harder time rousing them. The second day was worse than the first. On the third day, all hope deserted young Clemens.

Finally they came to a little inn. The inn was filled

with the worst kind of men, and it was apparent that even the slightest quarrel could lead to a deadly fight. Sam and Ballou ate some greasy rabbit stew and then went for a stroll to get out of the tense atmosphere.

Nearby, an Indian village was in the midst of hastily packing up and making off. Tepees were being disbanded, dogs were running underfoot, squaws were picking up pemmican and loading blankets on the horses. Everything was noise and confusion. It was obvious that the Indians were terrified of some evil, but Sam and Ballou were at a loss to make out what it was.

Sam, who was the braver of the two, tried to inquire what was the matter, but he could not get anyone to stop and explain. Finally a young brave took time out to point to the creek. "Much water," he said. "Soon."

Ballou and Sam thought the Indian was crazy. The creek was gentle and placid; there was nothing to be afraid of. It was no doubt the work of some medicine man who had a hidden reason for wanting the tribe to move on.

"Let's get some sleep," Sam proposed. "I'm dead."

The two men were hardly more than into their dreams back at the inn when there was a tremendous outcry. Horses were stamping in their stalls, the livestock was in a panic, and men were running, shouting, and cursing on all sides of them. Ballou, who thought that a gun battle had broken out, rushed to see what had happened. The Carson River had run rampant; there was water on all sides of them. By the time Sam and his friend got downstairs to see to their horses, they were sloshing along in water that lapped over their boots. In a few moments the men and animals were on higher ground;

the inn was a little island in the middle of all those rush-
ing waters.

The flood lasted a week, and Sam and his friends
were marooned at "Honey Lake Smith's," as the inn was
known. The whole seven days were a procession of swear-
ing, drinking, card-playing, and fighting, punctuated by
dirt and vermin.

By the eighth day the stream had gone down, but it
was still too swollen for a safe crossing. Nevertheless, Ollendorff, Ballou and Sam elected to attempt a crossing.
They were thoroughly fed up with the life at the inn.
They took off in a canoe; the horses attached to the stern.
The horses lost their footing and Ollendorff panicked,
fearing that the boat would upset and that the three men
would be swept to death in the strong current.

"We warned Ollendorff to keep his wits about him
and handle himself carefully," writes Sam in *Roughing
It,* "but it was useless; the moment the bow touched the
bank, he made a spring and the canoe whirled upside
down in ten-foot water. Ollendorff seized some brush and
dragged himself ashore, but Ballou and I had to swim
for it, encumbered with our overcoats. But we held on to
the canoe, and although we were washed down nearly to
Carson, we managed to push the boat ashore and make a
safe landing."

The horses were saved, too, but the two men were
soaked through, and it was no time of the year for such a
drenching. They had to bail out the canoe, and let horses,
men, and blankets dry out overnight before going on.

The next morning they left for Carson City regardless of the fact that a furious snow storm was blowing.
Ballou was dubious about the direction the three should

take, but "Ollendorff said his instinct was as sensitive as any compass, and that he could 'strike a bee-line' for Carson City and never diverge from it."

The trio started out in an unmarked white world, heads bent against the snow. After a while they sighted hoofprints and were encouraged. As they continued, the number of prints grew and grew. "We wondered," Sam says, "how so large a party came to be traveling at such a time and in such solitude. Somebody suggested that it must be a company of soldiers from the fort, and so we accepted that solution and jogged along a little faster still . . ."

Still they seemed to be making no progress. But the prints in the snow increased, as if the platoon of soldiers had expanded into a regiment. Finally Ballou reigned in his horse and looked down at the prints.

"Boys," he said, "these are our own tracks, and we've actually been circussing round and round in a circle for more than two hours, out here in this blind desert!"

After all their cold, hard travel, they were still in sight of the inn! The three men stood in the snow hesitating. They did not want to spend another night at Honey Lake Smith's, but they could not trust Ollendorff's "compass" either. While they were debating, the stagecoach forded the river, and the three men fell in line behind it. Although the fresh horses of the stage soon pulled it far ahead, the three men told themselves they could follow the tracks in the snow.

They continued for some time; then Sam noticed that the tracks were getting fainter and fainter; at last they ceased altogether. The snow had covered them.

Darkness fell and they were afraid to continue. The

only thing to do was to make camp, to try to get a fire going, and wait until morning. In their haste to leave Honey Lake Smith's, they had gone off half-prepared, and now they discovered that they had only four matches, Ballou having those, Sam and Ollendorff having none. The three gathered sagebrush and hopefully struck one match after another, trying to ignite the wet wood. When they had used up three, they began to panic, and in the ensuing confusion Sam let go of the reins of the horses, and the horses bolted.

The last match failed. They were now lost in the snow, it was dark and cold, and their horses had run off. They had no provisions, no blankets, no way of keeping warm. They knew that it was fatal to fall asleep but they could not keep their eyes open. Sam tried continually to rouse his two friends, but they gradually sank down in sleep. He went about, brushing snow off them, trying to make them wake up, but they slept, blanketed with snow. Then Sam felt himself slipping down into sleep. He could not stop his eyelids from closing and as he dozed off he remembered stories of other men who had given into the temptation to lay down in the warm snow and sleep, and who had frozen to death.

He awoke to hear Ballou shouting savagely. They had fallen into the snow only a few yards from a stage coach station. Their horses were standing by the shed. They had nearly died in what they thought was a wilderness when they need only to have walked five minutes for food, shelter, and warmth.

Chapter 9

Newspaperman

Sam went off, good as his word, to see what was happening at Esmeralda. He was twenty-six years old, he had a red beard, wore the usual floppy hat of the miner, had let his hair go long, and dressed in rough clothes and big boots. As a picturesque touch, he had a navy revolver tucked into his belt. Even though he could not shoot, he carried the gun as part of his dress. In the West a man would as soon be seen without pants as without a gun.

Most of the men who headed for Esmeralda were seeking their fortunes, a wild crew, used to sudden shootings, savage quarreling, and endless knifings. Fortunes were being made, lost, made, lost, made and lost. Men came into town paupers and went out millionaires, or came in millionaires and went out paupers. Many never left at all, but were buried in rude pine coffins and put in the little cemetery which seemed to grow as fast as the population. Aurora, eight miles from the Walker River, a ghost town today, was then humming with activity. It was a town founded on easy money—easy come, easy go— with all the lawless immorality that such loose money brings. Men came into riches too quick; they lost their sense of humility, and the feeling of being like other men.

They felt themselves above the law, and often took the law into their own hands. It was a city of men who knew no real law save the gun.

Women were few. There were no wives, only a scattering of dance hall girls. When a wagon train of settlers occasionally went through, the miners would rush out and stare, begging just to touch a dress that a woman wore. The sight of a child could reduce these hardened men to tears.

Afflicted with "gold fever"

The Esmeralda claim which Orion and Sam had invested in turned out to be more trouble than it was worth. Sam had made the trip with a man named Higbie, but Higbie was no better a miner than Sam. The two were understandably discouraged, but eventually Higbie located what he thought was a fortune in silver. The two filed their claim and were going to start in working it immediately, in accordance with the law which stated they *must* work their claim within ten days to hold onto it. Unfortunately, while Higbie was away Sam was called to tend a sick friend. Sam left a note for Higbie telling him to go ahead with the excavating. When Sam returned on the ninth day, he asked Higbie how much had been done.

Higbie looked at Sam in astonishment. "Didn't you get my note?" he demanded. Higbie then confessed that he had gone on to to see about another mine that he was sure would bring them a fortune. He had left a note for Sam, which Sam in his haste had missed. Their claim had not been worked and the two men lost it. It turned out later that the mine would have perhaps been worth a fortune for both men.

Sam's money, which he had saved from his steamboating days, was rapidly dwindling, and he was forced to take a job as a day laborer in a quartz mill. His wages were ten dollars a week and board—bacon, beans, coffee, bread, apples, and molasses. His working hours were from dawn to dusk, and one week was enough to convince him that he was not cut out for that kind of work.

But Sam had to make money. Earlier he had received a job offer from Joseph Goodman, editor of the *Territorial Enterprise,* and he now decided to go back to newspaper work.

Goodman knew Sam's work from occasional short sketches that Sam had sent him. Sam signed these humorous pieces "Josh," and the offer which came for "Josh's" work was for $25 a week, a lordly sum in Sam's present position.

Sam Clemens walked one hundred miles to Virginia City. He was through with mining and ready to make his fortune by writing. He had come to believe that the pen might be mightier than the pick axe.

When he arrived at the newspaper office, he was hot and tired, covered with dust and burdened down with clothing, blankets, a rucksack and canteen. His appearance was hardly one to inspire confidence, but in the West men had learned to judge a man not by his appearance but by the testing of his character. Clothes, in Virginia City, did not make the man. It did not take Sam long to prove himself worth all the confidence his articles had previouly inspired.

Virginia City was one of the toughest of the tough cities of the West, a lawless huddle of saloons, gambling houses, and other unsavory meeting places for criminals, horse thieves, rustlers, desperados, and drifters.

The town had fifteen thousand people, most of them unprincipled. But they were well suited to a town which hung on the edge of a mountain, and which looked as if it might slide down its mountainside at any moment. There was an ever-present danger, too, that the town might cave in. There was a whole beehive of tunnels under Virginia City where the miners had taken out earth and ore.

Virginia City, the town that silver had built, was a brassy, blaring town. Everyone was rich; everyone spent money like water. Even though the town was less than ten years old and had been built by rough miners and prospectors, there were hotels and theaters, plush bars and exotic dance halls.

The Comstock Lode had been discovered by two brothers, the Groshes, in 1857. The Grosh brothers were on their way to the California gold mines when they found the silver deposits. They died under tragic circumstances, but the mine had been recorded. News of the strike was not made public until 1859, however, when Henry Comstock, known as "Old Pancake," claimed the stake which now bears his name. Comstock had been a sheepherder and apparently had come upon the Grosh brothers' cabin and seen the record of their discovery. Comstock sold the claim for practically nothing. It was others who made a fortune out of his find.

The Comstock Lode was one of those unbelievable sources of silver that every miner dreams about. Under the houses of Virginia City, in the passageways and tunnels, men worked day and night excavating silver. In one year alone the lode yielded $36,000,000. The rich vein lasted twenty years; but in 1882 the bonanza came to an end. In a search for new riches, the shaft that had been sunk in Sutro Tunnel hit hot water and the mines were flooded.

The atmosphere in Virginia City when Sam Clemens arrived was unreal. Men seemed to have no idea what was occurring in the great nation that was growing all around them. They were self-centered, selfish men who cared only about easy wealth and nothing about the expansion of the great new nation that was daily moving farther and farther west. Although Oregon and California had already applied and been admitted to the Union, the rest of the territory of the West was still going through the growing pains of adolescence. It would be a long time before law and order had been imposed and a longer time before the territory was a safe place for men to bring up families.

In Virginia City almost no one spoke of the great Civil War; it was silver men talked of, silver and how to find it, how to hold on to it, and how to get the most for it. People went about in a daze of well-being, imagining themselves rich beyond counting when in reality they owned only portions of different mines, mines that might—or might not—strike rich ore. Friends gave mining shares away freely, and if a man needed money, he sold some of his stock; if not, he kept his shares, imagining his riches to be beyond computing.

"The sidewalks swarmed with people—to such an extent, indeed, that it was generally no easy matter to stem the human tide," Sam Clemens wrote in *Roughing It*. "The streets themselves were just as crowded with quartz-wagons, freight-teams, and other vehicles. The procession was endless. So great was the pack, that buggies frequently had to wait half an hour for an opportunity to cross the principal street . . . Money was as plenty as dust; every individual considered himself wealthy, and a melancholy countenance was nowhere to be seen. There were military companies, fire companies, brass-bands, banks, hotels, theaters, 'hurdy-gurdy houses,' wide-open gambling palaces, political pow-wows, civic processions, street-fights, inquests, riots, a whisky-mill every fifteen steps . . . a dozen breweries, and half a dozen jails and station-houses in full operation, and some talk of building a church."

The paper, the *Territorial Enterprise,* had been a

bankrupt weekly journal when Goodman came to the city. He had bought it for two hundred and fourteen dollars. Now the paper had five editors and twenty-three compositors. It cost subscribers sixteen dollars a year, and it had more advertising than it could take care of. Now a daily newspaper, it was clearing six thousand dollars a month, and to Sam it was an unbelievable success after his experience with the little papers of Missouri and Iowa. Goodman, the editor, had found a silver mine in his newspaper every bit as rich as the one that ran underneath his presses.

Sam, who was assigned to do a daily column on local happenings, discovered that the Virginia City notion of justice was somewhat limited. Although there were trials for murder, the jury was usually made up of desperados, and it was usually impossible to get a conviction. Sam chafed at the instances of injustice he saw on all sides of him.

Meanwhile, news came to Sam that Captain Sellers, that bombastic old man who had first used the name of Mark Twain, had died. Sam remembered the satire he had written years before and was ashamed anew that he had hurt the old man. Hearing of Sellers made him remember many times, happy times, back on the great Mississippi. In his sleep at night he heard again the call, "M-a-r-k three! M-a-r-k three! Quarter-less-three! Half twain! Quarter twain! M-a-r-k twain." He decided that if he used the name Mark Twain he would be making amends to the old riverboat captain in his own way, and from this time on he signed all his articles "Mark Twain." It was to become one of the most famous names in American literature. But even more important, a new man was beginning to take shape. Where Sam Clemens of Hannibal, Missouri, had been closely associated with a certain way of life, now Mark Twain, a writer whose humor and wit reached out to all the world, was beginning to emerge. In a sense, Sam Clemens had stopped being Sam Clemens. From this point on he was Mark Twain.

The humorous, chatty pieces of Mark Twain were so highly praised that his salary was soon raised fifteen dollars a week. And Goodman thought so highly of him that he asked Mark to serve as acting editor when Goodman had to make a trip to San Francisco. While Goodman was away, Mark wrote an article attacking the editor of the rival paper, the *Virginia Union*. The editor was so incensed that he demanded that his honor be vindicated in the way of the West, by a duel.

Mark had little idea how to conduct a duel, and he sought the advice of his friends. In his *Autobiography* he recalled the advice that was given to him. ". . . the correct position for the gun—that the position ordinarily in use at Virginia City (that is to say, the gun straight up in the air, then brought slowly down to your man) was all wrong. At the word *'One,'* you must raise the gun slowly and steadily to the place on the other man's body that you desire to convince. Then, after a pause, *'Two, three—fire—Stop!'* At the word 'stop,' you may fire—but not earlier. You may give yourself as much time as you please *after* that word. Then, when you fire, you may advance and go on firing at your leisure and pleasure, if you can get any pleasure out of it. And, in the meantime, the other man, if he has been properly instructed and is alive to his privileges, is advancing on *you,* and firing—and it is always likely that more or less trouble will result . . . Take all the risks of getting murdered yourself but don't run any risk of murdering the other man. If you survive a duel you want to survive in such a way that the memory of it will not linger along with you the rest of your life and interfere with your sleep. Aim at your man's leg; not at the knee, not above the knee, for those are dangerous spots. Aim below the knee; cripple him but leave the rest of him to his mother."

Mark remembered the man who had been shot during his brief time with the Confederate forces. He thought of that stranger, killed so meaninglessly, and he remembered his vow that he would not shoot again unless he had to. Yet he knew that honor demanded that he see the duel through.

News of the coming duel went through town like wild fire. There was a new law which said there was to be no dueling, and while Mark Twain was debating the course of his action, the governor sent word to him that the new law would be enforced. If Mark went through with the duel, he would receive a sentence of two years' imprisonment. Mark was now in the untenable position of having to beg off the duel and lose his honor or going through with it and serving two years in prison. The governor had also sent word that there was a stage leaving at four the next morning. Mark took the hint, and with a friend, Steve Gillis, he caught the Overland coach to San Francisco on a Spring morning in 1864.

Chapter 10

Off To Hawaii

Mark's destination was California. He was disturbed about his abrupt departure from Virginia City, but he was comforted by the belief that he was carrying a suit-case containing shares of mining stock which made him, on paper, worth a fortune. Much of the stock had been given to him by friends. It was the custom in Virginia City for a prospector to pass out shares of his latest claim to friends. Mark, with his capacity for making people like him, had accumulated a large number of shares in various mines.

In San Francisco he went to the finest hotel and spent his money lavishly. He lived as befit a young man who was worth a fortune in silver. Every day the stock market showed that his investments were soaring; he was getting richer and richer. Then, suddenly, the figures began to drop. They went down faster and faster; in a short time he had lost everything. His fortune had existed on paper alone, and when he had paid his hotel bills he had exactly fifty dollars to his name.

He was thirty years old and he had nothing to show for his years. He had set out to make the world know his mark. He had planned to go exploring on the Amazon; he had prospected for silver; he had worked for newspapers, and he had been the admired, envied pilot of a

Mississippi steamboat. As he now looked at his past, he asked himself what in reality he had accomplished. Nothing, nothing. He had no money and no fame. No one knew the name Sam Clemens, or Mark Twain, save a few miners who would soon forget it. He was merely another down-and-out miner with a story of past riches, that were gone. He was like other has-beens he had once pitied, written about, and thought of no more.

Depressed though he was, San Francisco fascinated him. It was a fabulous town founded on the profits of catering to gold miners. It was in 1848 that James Q. Marshall had discovered gold at the site of a sawmill he was building for Johann Sutter in the Sacramento Valley. In no time at all the '49ers were pouring into California. San Francisco grew fast as a boom city, and its riotous and lawless Barbary Coast was infamous throughout the nation. Finally members of the community took the law into their own hands. A Committee of Vigilantes was formed, people who set out to suppress violence and lawlessness until a regularly established government could take over control.

When the gold rush started, the California territory had already been agitating for statehood. In 1850 it was admitted to the Union as a state. Four years later the great gold bonanza began to dwindle, and the state began to settle down to an ordinary progress toward a reasonable, sane existence.

When Mark Twain arrived in San Francisco, the city was well on its way to becoming one of the most distinctive cities in America. The glorious view across the bay, the profusion of flowers, and the rapidly expanding city appealed to the young man. Here were palaces the rich had erected on the heights of the city, here were elegantly dressed men and women, here, too, were men of culture and discernment.

Steve Gillis and Mark were soon working for the *San Francisco Morning Call,* Mark as a reporter, Steve as a compositor.

But Mark soon discovered that greed, graft and corruption were just as rampant here in San Francisco as they had been in Virginia City. He longed to expose the worse elements of the city, but he found he could not always be as outspoken as he wished. As the weeks passed, his interest waned and he realized that he would not be able to launch his attacks openly as long as he worked for a San Francisco newspaper. Finally Goodman agreed to take him on as the San Francisco correspondent for the Virginia City *Territorial Enterprise.* Immediately Mark launched a series of articles in which he poured out all his loathing for the corruption in the San Francisco government.

Naturally those he attacked were not pleased. But they bided their time until they could get something on him. Mark was warned again and again, but he continued his articles.

Mark's friend, Steve Gillis, was arrested and Mark went bail for him. Steve, hearing that he would not have a fair trial, fled from San Francisco, and Mark was held responsible for Steve's jumping bail. Mark knew he would not get fair treatment from the authorities, so on the advice of friends, he, too, left town and went off to hide out with Steve's brother, Jim.

The men who owned the cabin where Mark stayed were miners. As he watched the pocket miners panning gold every day, Mark's dream of making a fortune returned. He watched the men patiently put dirt through a sieve and retrieve the nuggets that were left after the dirt had been washed away with water. He forgot all his old resolutions and tried this new way of mining. But at last he was once more convinced that any type of mining was hopeless for him.

Back in San Francisco a change in the officialdom made his position better, and he again went to work for Goodman's paper. But his restlessness made him dissatisfied and he was soon looking about for new territories to conquer. He had gone, he thought, as far West as he could go; he was backed up to the Pacific Ocean now, but even an ocean wasn't enough to stop Mark Twain. Soon he was formulating plans to make a trip to the Hawaiian Islands, then called the Sandwich Islands. He would write a series of newspaper articles to pay his way.

On March 17, 1866, Mark Twain boarded the *Ajax* and started off across the Pacific. He had an arrangement to write four letters a month for twenty dollars a piece; he had his passage on the *Ajax* free, and he was going two thousand miles to an island paradise.

Kamehameha V was the king of the islands, grandson of the great Kamehameha who had unified the islands and established a strong, vigorous dynasty. The arrival in the 1820s, over forty years before, of missionaries had changed conditions on the islands. The use of human sacrifice, the strong, powerful, often cruel feudal system which had grown up, and the undisputed power of a minority over the vast majority of the people, was at an end.

The Hawaiians were said to be a good-natured, courteous, happy people, and their present ruler an enlightened monarch. Education was on the move. Before the arrival of the missionaries, the Hawaiians had had no written language, all their history and customs having been handed down from generation to generation by a few specially trained men. But the missionaries had produced a vocabulary and arranged to have books printed. Now the Hawaiians were becoming part of the modern life of the nineteenth century.

Sam's first sight after two thousand miles of sea was the view of Diamond Head rising out of the ocean. Then Waikiki Beach came into view, and finally the famed coconut trees, and the shining white town of Honolulu. It was like a vision of Paradise. Everywhere were blankets of flowers and tapestries of bright green shrubs. Standing over the lazy sea and misty surf were great shining trees. Oranges, pineapples, bananas, strawberries, lemons, limes, mangoes, guavas and melons grew in profusion.

Hawaii was like nothing Mark Twain had ever seen and it was everything that he had always dreamed a "foreign" place should be. Pearl Harbor with its strange, lush, tropical beauty seemed to him the most beautiful, peaceful place in the world. The mode of life in Honolulu was a revelation: there was no harried scramble for money, rather people moved slowly, enjoying food and friendship, and spending hours outdoors enjoying the natural beauties that surrounded them.

Mark Twain found that he could work freely and easily, and much of the tenseness that haunted him in San Francisco now left. He contemplated the greed and corruption which he had witnessed in the West and which had worried him for months with a detached view.

[111]

All his interest was kindled. He busied himself going everywhere, trying to see everything, writing about his experiences and sending off his articles. One of the things that he most wanted to see was the great volcano of Kilauea. The crater was reputed to be ten miles in circumference and in some places over a thousand feet deep.

Mark Twain started after dark and went up the side of the crater. He could see the glare from the fires and smoke clouds rising above the volcano. In the crater itself there were flames belching tongues of fire. The guides refused to go further, but Mark Twain was determined to see everything.

A stranger approached and volunteered to show him the way. The stranger, who introduced himself as Marlette, said he knew a path across the crater and the two "skipped over the hot floor and over the red crevices with brisk despatch and reached the cold lava safe but with pretty warm feet," Mark later wrote. When they got near the boiling fire, he thought they were "in a gloomy desert, and a suffocatingly dark one, surrounded by dim walls that seemed to tower to the sky."

Suddenly Marlette shouted "Stop!" Mark Twain needed no second command. Marlette said they were off the path and that they were in the midst of beds of rotten lava. If they took a wrong step, they might plunge a thousand feet through the ash to their deaths. At that point Marlette moved gingerly forward and went crashing through the ash and disappeared to his waist. Considerably shaken, he managed to get out and the two men crept forward carefully.

"The lava surface was all alike in the lantern-light,"

Mark Twain wrote, and Marlette said "it was not the lantern that had informed him that we were out of the path, but *his* feet." Marlette had noticed that the lava-needles made a peculiar grinding sound underfoot and now he put the light behind him and searched with his feet instead of his eyes. When he did not hear that peculiar grinding sound, he knew he was on the right path again. The two men reached the North Lake of the volcano after a long hike, and the glare "was so blinding that it was some time before we could bear to look upon it steadily. It was like gazing at the sun at noonday, except the glare was not quite so white. At unequal distances all around the shores of the lake were nearly white-hot chimneys or hollow drums of lava, four or five feet high, and up through them were bursting gorgeous sprays of lava gouts and gem spangles, some white, some red, and some golden . . ."

Mark Twain was completely worn out by the time he got back to Honolulu, and he was advised to take a rest or he might suffer serious effects from all his strenuous endeavors. While he was resting, the survivors of *Hornet* ship disaster came in. The *Hornet* had burned at sea and the survivors, with rations for only ten days, had been at sea for forty-three days. An open boat with fifteen men more dead than alive drifted into the harbor of Honolulu. The four-thousand-mile voyage that had taken them to Honolulu had crazed most of them.

Mark Twain insisted on getting up from his sick bed and interviewing the survivors. He was too ill to go on foot, but his stubbornness won the day. He had himself carried on a stretcher to see the survivors. Then he interviewed each, rushed home, and wrote all night the story of that fateful trip, finishing just in time to get the packet with his news aboard the *Ajax*.

His vivid, sympathetic tales of the survivors and his impassioned account of the disaster, as well as the fact that he had been the first to get the news back to America, made him famous. Although the dispatches had originally been sent only to two papers, the *Union* of Sacramento and his old friend Goodman of the *Enterprise*,

Carried on a stretcher to get the news

most of the important papers in America picked up the stories. Readers all over the country became familiar with his name.

He was in Hawaii altogether five months. When he returned, he decided to lecture on his experiences, and he hired the San Francisco Opera House for his talk. He bought newspaper space to advertise: "Admission one dollar; doors open at half past seven, the trouble begins at eight." He was absolutely certain no one would turn up, and he went to the hall in a mood of deepest despair. He was flabbergasted to find that the auditorium was jammed. His lecture was a great success, and all the San Francisco papers reported his triumph in detail. After this one evening, he decided to arrange a lecture tour through the West.

He lectured for three weeks in California and Nevada, and he made more silver at humorous talk than he had ever made in mining.

But finally he felt the time had come for him to return East. He took a boat for New York, and the trip was one of terror and tragedy. Cholera broke out shortly after the boat left port, and there were many burials at sea. But disregarding personal danger, he volunteered his services and helped nurse the sick.

Chapter 11

Europe and the Holy Land

Mark Twain was afraid that no one would know him in New York, that a Westerner in the big city would sink like a pebble in the middle of a pond. Frank Fuller, an old friend from the West, helped him to arrange a lecture. The tickets sold slowly at first, and even Fuller began to lose his enthusiasm. Finally the two men decided to get in touch with every Californian they knew and to make each one promise to come. The Californians were a loyal contingent, and they flooded the hall on the night of May 6th. When Mark walked on the platform, he was greeted by a storm of applause.

His lecturing a success, he began to cast about for some new way to use his talents. He heard of a boat that was going to make a tour of Europe and the Holy Land, and he hit upon the idea of joining the group and writing about their experiences. The *Quaker City* was a coal burning, side-wheel propellered ship with sails. The cruise was advertised as a luxury one and the fare was $1,250 per person. Mark talked some newspapers into buying his dispatches, he secured passage on the ship, and awaited excitedly its departure.

His first day aboard was a disappointment. Most of the people on the *Quaker City*, Mark noted with a sinking heart, were well advanced in years. There was one young fellow, however, Charles Langdon, from Elmira, New York, who seemed lively and entertaining. The two spent many hours together and one evening, just before dinner, Mark wandered into Langdon's cabin and sighted the picture of a lovely young girl. "Your fiancée?" he asked curiously. "She certainly is a beauty."

"It's my sister," Langdon said, "And she is a beauty and more than a beauty, the nicest, kindest, sweetest girl in the whole world."

Most of the tourists on the *Quaker City* were strongly religious and Mark found his rough Western ways often difficult to suppress. Nevertheless, he was considered a famous figure because of his newspaper articles and his lectures, and most of the passengers were content to make allowances for his behavior. The passengers themselves amused and amazed him, and he took great fun in writing about their foibles and their peculiarities.

The anecdotes and experiences of Mark's trip to Europe and the Holy Land were later collected in a book called *Innocents Abroad*. Perhaps the funniest and most celebrated of the anecdotes are those in which Mark Twain tells about his troubles with European guides. Guides were necessary in Europe, he found, but he found also that the guides took half the pleasure out of the sights by always expecting unrestrained enthusiasm from the tourists.

After a time Mark Twain and a small circle of his companions got tired of having to admire extravagantly every painting and piece of statuary, every historical place and famous house, to say nothing of churches and museums, famous palaces and scenic spots. After a time the party made a pact *never* to show any enthusiasm for anything, no matter how much they might admire it.

The doctor in the party was particularly adept at exasperating the guides with his indifference. He would patiently and doggedly ask one ridiculous question after another—all without showing the slightest emotion. And he could put more imbecility into his face, Mark Twain wrote, than any other man alive.

The guides in Genoa were particularly happy to get American tourists because Genoa contained so much that was associated with Christopher Columbus. The guide assigned to Mark Twain's party was fidgeting with animation and impatience thinking of the wonders he would show them.

"Come wis me, genteelmen!—come! I show you ze letter writing by Christopher Colombo!" he said. "Write it himself!—write it with his own hand!—come!"

The guide spent a long time fumbling with his keys opening locks to get the letters, trying to heighten the tourists' impatience. By the time he had the letter he was beside himself, dancing about them, looking in first one face, then another, sure of his triumph. "What I tell you, genteelmen! Is it not? See!" he crowed. "Handwriting Christopher Colombo!—write it himself."

Mark Twain and his friends stood looking indifferent and unconcerned. The doctor picked up the letter and looked at it a long time, examining it carefully, never once revealing an ounce of enthusiasm. Finally he said, "What—what did you say was the name of the party who wrote this?"

"Christopher Colombo! ze great Christopher Colombo!"

The doctor went on looking at the letter without expression. Finally he glanced up and said, "Ah—did he write it himself, or—or how?"

"He write it himself!" the guide explained, dancing up and down in impatience. "Christopher Colombo! he's own handwriting, write it by himself."

Then the doctor laid the document down and said, "Why, I have seen boys in America only fourteen years old that could write better than that."

The guide seemed unable to believe what his ears had heard. "But zis is ze great Christo—" he began.

"I don't care who it is!" the doctor said indignantly. "It's the worst writing I ever saw. Now you mustn't think you can impose on us because we are strangers. We are not fools, by a good deal. If you have got any specimens of penmanship of real merit, trot them out!—and if you haven't, drive on."

The guide would not give up. At last he said, "Ah, genteelmen, you come wis me! I show you beautiful, oh, magnificent bust Christopher Colombo!—splendid, grand, magnificent!"

He took them to see the bust, and Mark Twain says it was beautiful. But not one of the *Quaker City* party allowed a single expression of interest to betray his real emotion. The doctor put on his glasses and stared blankly at the statue. "Ah—what did you say this gentleman's name was?" he asked.

"Christopher Colombo!" the guide screamed. "Ze great Christopher Colombo!"

"Christopher Colombo—the great Christopher Colombo. Well, what did *he do?*"

"Discover America!—discover America, oh, ze devil!"

"Discover America," the doctor repeated. "No—that statement will hardly wash. We are just from America ourselves. We heard nothing about it. Christopher Colombo—pleasant name—is—is he dead?"

"Oh, *corpo di Baccho!*" moaned the guide. "Three hundred year!"

"What did he die of?" the doctor asked, showing a little interest.

"I do not know!—I cannot tell."

"Smallpox, think?"

"I do not know, genteelmen!—I do not know *what* he die of!"

"Measles, likely?"

"Maybe—maybe—I do *not* know—I think he die of somethings."

The doctor looked at the guide expressionlessly. "Parents living?" he asked.

"Im-posseeble!"

"Ah—which is the bust and which is the pedestal?"

"Santa Maria!" the guide exclaimed in despair. "*Zis* ze bust!—zis ze pedestal!"

In Rome the party was taken to see a royal Egyptian mummy, the best-preserved in the world, the guide said. By this time some of the guide's old enthusiasm had come back because he was certain he had something that would interest his charges. "See, genteelmen!—Mummy! Mummy!" he exclaimed happily.

The doctor took out his eyeglass calmly. "What did I understand you to say the gentleman's name was?"

"Name?—he got no name!—Mummy!—'Gyptian mummy!"

"Yes, yes," the doctor agreed. "Born here?"

"No! 'Gyptian mummy!"

"Ah, just so. Frenchman, I presume?"

"No!—not Frenchman, not Roman!—born in Egypta!"

"Is, ah—is he dead?"

"Born in Egypta," the doctor said. "Never heard of Egypta before. Foreign locality likely. Mummy—mummy. How calm he is—how self-possessed." The doctor looked at the guide. He asked with an absolutely still, solemn face, "Is, ah—is he dead?"

The guide went white. But he did manage to tell them that the mummy had been dead some three thousand years.

The doctor turned on him savagely. "Here, now," he said, "what do you mean by such conduct as this! Playing us for Chinamen because we are strangers and trying to learn! Trying to impose your vile second-hand

[121]

carcasses on *us!*—thunder and lightning, I've a notion to—to—if you've got a nice *fresh* corpse, fetch him out! —or, by George, we'll brain you!"

From that point on the little group found that there was one remark which never failed to undo their guides. They always used it whenever they could think of nothing else to say. After the guide had exhausted their patence in praising the beauty of some ancient bronze image or a famous broken-legged statue, the party would look on stupidly, silent for five, ten, fifteen minutes, for as long as all of them could hold out, until one of them would ask, "Is, ah—is he dead?"

Later in the trip the pilgrims met the liberal and humane Russian Emperor, Alexander II, who afterwards was assassinated in St. Petersburg by the explosion of bombs planted by Nihilists. The Emperor and his Empress were charming people and friendly to Americans. They spoke English fluently, and were cultivated and artistic in temperament.

The party of sixty-five pilgrims aboard the *Quaker City* was wild with excitement when the invitation came requesting that the passengers be guests of their Majesties. The monarchs were staying at a summer palace, quite small, so it was decided that the reception would be held in the gardens—the gentlemen to wear swallow-tail coats, white kid gloves, and white neckties; and the ladies to dress in light-colored silks.

The reception was a resounding success. Both the Russian czar and his wife were delightfully informal, moving among the Americans with smiles and small chatter, and scarcely standing at all on the trappings of their official positions. To Mark Twain the naturalness and the simplicity of the Russian Emperor and his wife was a great revelation. He hated pomp and circumstance; to see how naturally royalty could act showed him a side of monarchy that he had not suspected. He was quite won over by the imperial family, particularly by the fourteen-year-old daughter of the family, whose sweetness and charm impressed everyone.

After the Emperor and his wife showed the pilgrims through the palace, they sent them on to the Crown Prince's palace, where a "breakfast" was served. There was bread and cheese, an assortment of cold meats, tea and two kinds of wine. The *Quaker City* passengers helped themselves in picnic fashion and ate on the lawns.

"I had supposed," writes Mark Twain, a staunch supporter of democracy, "that Emperors were terrible people. I thought they never did anything but wear magnificent crowns and red velvet dressing-gowns with dabs of wool sewed on them in spots, and sit on thrones and scowl at flunkies and the people in the parquette, and order Dukes and Duchesses off to execution. I find, however, that when one is so fortunate as to get behind the scenes and see them at home and in the privacy of their firesides, they are strangely like common mortals. They are pleasanter to look upon then than they are in their theatrical aspect. It seems to come as natural to them to dress and act like other people as it is to put a friend's cedar pencil in your pocket when you are done using it."

But he could not pass up the opportunity of course of poking a little fun at the world at large and himself in particular. "But," he continued, "I can never have any confidence in the tinsel kings of the theater after this. It will be a great loss. I used to take such a thrilling pleasure in them. But, hereafter, I will turn me sadly away and say:

"This does not answer—this isn't the style of king that *I* am acquainted with.

"When they swagger around the stage in jeweled crowns and splendid robes, I shall beel bound to observe that all the Emperors that ever *I* was personally acquainted with wore the commonest sort of clothes, and did not swagger."

The pilgrims finally reached their long-sought destination, the Holy Land. Mark Twain—one of a small group of eight—elected to take the long trip from Syria, by Baalbek to Damascus, the oldest city in the world, and from there on down to Palestine. It would be a long, hot trip and fatiguing, for the entire journey was to be made by horseback.

In Beirut, the men prepared for their trip. Shortly after six one morning the pack-train appeared. There were nineteen serving-men and twenty-six pack-mules as well as the mounts for the eight men and the dragoman who was to lead the way.

Twain could not understand what all those men and animals were needed for, but at the end of the first day he discovered that a pack train in Palestine was different from a pack train in Nevada. There were five large tents of blue and gold and crimson, all splendidly ornamented. There were eight little iron bedsteads inside the tents on which soft downy mattresses and pillows were placed, these covered by sparkling white linen. There was a table about the centerpole with pitchers, basins, soap, and white towels, a set for each man, and—unbelievable as it seemed—carpets were even spread on the floor.

At night candles were placed on the tables in the tents and the room glowed with warm, cozy light reflected in the highly-polished brass candlesticks. There was even a "main" tent, where the men dined on food of the finest quality, much better than they had been accustomed to at the best hotels of the cities along the Mediterranean. They ate mutton, chicken, and goose all roasted to perfection; and potatoes, bread, tea, pudding, apples, and grapes. These lavish feasts were served from the best plates, with snowy white tablecloths and fresh napkins. The servants were "stately fellows in baggy trousers and turbaned fezes," Twain recounted.

Needless to say, Mark Twain slept soundly that first night, and when the dragoman's bell sang out at five-thirty the next morning, he was ready to go. When he dressed and came out, scarcely ten minutes later, all the tents had been stripped and most of the equipment packed up. Yet the travelers were served hot mutton chops, fried chicken, omelettes, fried potatoes, and coffee for breakfast. By the time they had finished their second cup of coffee, the entire "village" had disappeared and the caravan was ready to move on.

The trip grew more strenuous the closer they came to the Holy City. There were many terrible days of traveling for twelve and thirteen hours under a burning sun without a bit of shade. The party began to feel as if it had been roasted in saddle, but it gallantly made on, passing one after another of the famous places of the Bible and gazing on those spots with wonder and awe.

There was no joking or poking fun at the guide now; all was solemnity and respect.

But even the seriousness of the occasion could not dull Mark's awareness of the humorous aspects of the group decked out in its various preposterous outfits to guard against the sun. Mark Twain was sure that they presented a spectacle the East would never forget. The eight traveled in single file; they all wore "the endless white rag of Constantinople wrapped round and round their hats and dangling down their backs"; they had thick green eyeglasses with sides to protect their eyes from the sun, and they held white umbrellas lined with green over their heads. Their stirrups were too short and they rode like no horsemen he had ever seen, with the horses trotting at a fearful gait and the rider bounding this way and that, "knees well up and stiff, elbows flapping like a rooster's that is going to crow, and the long file of umbrellas popping convulsively up and down."

All the members of the *Quaker City* were reunited in the Holy City, and the eight reluctantly abandoned their desert dress and went back to ordinary clothes. The pilgrims conducted themselves well on the whole, but they had two habits which nearly drove Mark Twain out of his natural good humor and tolerance.

Someone was endlessly scratching his name, his city, and the initials "U.S.A." on every monument that the group visited. Others had a habit of chipping off or digging up remnants of the monuments they visited. The destruction was prodigious, but there seemed to be no way to stop fools from putting their names in public places or from carting off parts of the sacred monument they had come thousand of miles to pay their respects to.

"The pilgrims," he states, "took down portions of the front walls for their specimens, as is their honored custom, and then departed."

The trip provided Mark Twain with a chance to poke fun at what he would have called "humbug." He detested pompousness, hogwash, romantic nonsense, and the worship of art which was not understood but merely venerated because it was old. Much of what he saw he considered a "swindle," and he did not hesitate to say so, but he never hesitated to poke fun at himself as well as at the other "innocents."

European customs bothered the democratic, individualistic man in Mark Twain, and he often scoffed at the undue reverence that was shown for the past. On the other hand, for the things that he genuinely appreciated, there was no more devoted admirer than Mark Twain.

At a time when Americans were first starting to make trips abroad, he captured a good deal of the cultural ignorance and crudeness of the citizens of this new nation. His passengers were, in truth, innocents, and he showed them as such—much to everyone's enjoyment and amusement.

Chapter 12

Livy and Love

After he returned to America, Mark Twain had a number of job offers but as always, he wanted to try something new. Doing what he had done before wasn't enough, he liked the challenge of new experiences, new ideas, new conquests. While he was trying to make up his mind whether or not to go back to newspaper work, he received a letter from the American Publishing Company of Hartford asking him if he had thought of collecting his newspaper sketches together in a book. The idea excited him and he began gathering his material for a book he called, *Innocents Abroad*.

That Christmas, Charles Langdon came down to New York and invited Sam to come to his hotel and meet his family. "Your sister is with them?" Mark asked eagerly, remembering the picture he had seen on the *Quaker City*.

Langdon laughed. "Yes," he said, "But don't think you or anyone else has a chance. She's always been frail and I guess we've spoiled her. But one thing is certain: she's spoiled us. We wouldn't dream of letting her go away with anyone."

Two days before Christmas Sam met the one and only woman in his life, Olivia Langdon. He had been invited to dinner and the moment he walked through the door he knew that his fate was set. One look at Livy confirmed the fact that she was everything Charles Langdon had said and more.

Olivia was very small and fragile, partially bedridden from an accident she had suffered on ice when she was sixteen. At the time that Mark Twain met her, she was twenty-two with enormous dark eyes in which the depth of her nature was mirrored. The rest of her features were small and patrician. She wore her jet black hair parted in the center and looped behind her neck in a large, glistening coil that seemed to hang, like a great black pearl, on the nape of her neck. Her skin was pale and white; she moved with grace and quietness, a small, shy figure in an enormous hooped skirt.

Mark Twain was awkward and intimidated at first, thinking himself an uncultured Westerner among the civilized Easterners. But gradually his warm, expansive nature opened up and he soon had the whole table laughing at his anecdotes. Everyone but Livy, that is. She kept looking at him as if he were some strange specimen out of a rodeo.

Charles Dickens, the noted British writer, author of *A Tale of Two Cities, David Copperfield,* and many other well-known books, was giving a reading that night, and the Langdon family invited Mark to accompany them to the lecture hall. Mark was intrigued by the consummate acting of Dickens who, dressed in a black velvet jacket with a pert flower at his buttonhole, seemed to Mark Twain everything that he was not. Mark was the free, exhuberant, uninhibited, sometimes vulgar but always

Cupid's darts

honest spirit of America; Dickens was the cultured, cultivated, polished, English man-of-letters.

Sitting in the darkened lecture hall, Mark began to feel his own inadequacies. How could he make the girl sitting next to him love him for what he was? She was used to fancy dandies, like her brother and father—good men, of course, but different—like Charles Dickens up there on the platform. He, Mark Twain, was only a man who spoke his mind, even when it would have been better to keep silent, and he knew he would never change. Even for Livy. But he had to have her, that much he knew, too. The question was how.

He felt he was making some progress when he received an invitation to make the New Year's Day call at a friend's house where the Langdon family was receiving guests. He and Livy's brother, Charles, arrived at eleven in the morning, and although it seemed that the moments flew by, he stayed more than twelve hours, not leaving until after midnight!

Mark Twain was now determined to finish his book and to make it as good as he could so that he could prove to Livy that he was worthy of her love. He had a job in Washington as secretary to Senator William Stewart, but he found the chores tedious and the work uninspiring. More and more he devoted his time to polishing up his book. Then an unexpected blow fell: the publishers of a paper in California had had his series of letters copyrighted and they notified him that *they* were going to bring out a book of those letters.

Mark Twain was thunder struck. But Colonel John McComb, the editor of the *Alta California,* showed the spirit of the West, the spirit of decency which was to characterize the new states, once they were free of lawless elements. Colonel McComb, even though he knew the paper would lose a great deal of money and even though the owners said the letters belonged to the paper, followed the dictates of his conscience. Without regard for his job and knowing that he was taking an unpopular position with his employers, he said that Mark Twain was right, the letters ought to belong to him. They were, after all, his work. After Colonel McComb's voice was raised in opposition to his own employers, other voices joined in. Finally Mark was allowed to use the material for his own book. The book was finished in July of that year—1869.

Tired but triumphant, Mark used his first freedom from work to make a trip to Elmira to visit the Langdon family. He was so excited at the prospect of seeing Livy he seemed not to be able to think about anything else. When Charles Langdon met him at the station, he was appalled at Mark's appearance.

Odd Western clothes or not, Mark was warmly welcomed by Mr. and Mrs. Langdon. But Olivia was polite and no more. No matter what enticements Mark used to try to win her around, she remained aloof—polite but distant. Charley finally confided to Mark that he wasn't giving her a chance. He had been so busy talking about himself and trying to make a good impression that Olivia hadn't been able to say a word!

Considerably chastened, Mark then fell into a glum silence. At the end of three days it was obvious to everyone that he was wildly, hopelessly in love with Olivia, and the Langdons were upset. The Langdons could not have been more different from the people Mark Twain had known. The Langdons were sternly practicing Congregationalists who thought of tobacco and alcohol as the sins of the fallen. They regarded strong language as the sign of the devil. Mark had been known to be friendly with all three.

Nevertheless, they liked Mark well enough—but as Charles's friend, not as Livy's suitor. Mr. Langdon finally spoke to him, trying to be kind, but telling him that his suit was hopeless.

In despair Mark made arrangements to leave. At the door he thought he detected looks of relief on all the faces about him, and he felt that if he left them in this state he would never get another invitation from the Langdon's. But what was he to do? It was obvious that they were all glad he was going. Charles was at the door. Mark pressed Livy's hand warmly; she smiled but took a step back.

No, there was nothing to do. The coach was waiting to take him to the station. He stepped up on the open step and into the coach behind the driver. He and Charles were waving goodby and at that instant the horse shied, bolted, and gave the carriage a violent jolt. The seat was loose, the two men were thrown to the floor.

Mark was dazed but no more. For a moment he lay still trying to collect his wits. Then he heard Charles saying, "Are you hurt? Hurt bad? Man, answer me, are you all right?"

I'm saved, Mark Twain thought. "I don't know," he said in the weakest voice he could counterfeit. "I feel— feel all funny. I don't *think* there's anything broken." The next instant all the family was crowded worriedly beside him, assuring him that he could not now make his journey back, that he must come in the house and they would call a doctor. It took Mark Twain two weeks to recover from that little bump and he left Elmira at the end of that time feeling that he had a pretty good chance of claiming the heart of the girl he loved.

One way he had thought to impress Olivia was to have her help him in saving himself. He presented himself to her as one of the fallen who might still be saved, and he let her know it was her "duty" to save souls—his in particular. He asked her if she would write letters of encouragement to him while he was away. His answers to her pious epistles on salvation showed a great deal more than just a friendly interest in the state of his soul.

In 1868 he took to lecturing again, using the material from his voyage to the Holy Land. He had a chance, since of one of his lecture dates was near Elmira, to stop by the house again. This time he pressed his suit earnestly and Mr. Langdon agreed to *consider* it. He asked Mark for a list of people who would testify that his character was honorable and that he would be a good husband for Livy. Mark gave him the names of several influential people he knew—men he knew not too well but whose names he thought would impress Mr. Langdon and who would not be too hard on him in giving character references since they knew him only slightly.

In January of the following year he went back to Elmira with high hopes. He had been writing Olivia constantly and had reason to believe that she had begun to return his affections.

But it was a glum Mr. Langdon who greeted him. They were no sooner in the living room together than Mr. Langdon asked for a private conference with Mark in the library. All of the so-called character references had written letters violently attacking Mark and warning the Langdon family against him. Two of the writers announced their belief that Mark Twain was headed for a drunkard's grave, and the other four were blackly pessimistic. When Mr. Langdon confronted the lover with this so-called objective opinion, he said, "What kind of people are these? Haven't you a friend in the world?"

"Apparently not."

"I'll be your friend myself. Take the girl. I know you better than they do."

Later Livy's father heard her new fiance talking of Joe Goodman of the *Territorial Enterprise*. Mr. Langdon asked if Goodman was a particular friend, and Mark Twain replied that he was the best one he ever had.

"Why, then," said Mr. Langdon, "what could you have been thinking of? Why didn't you refer me to him?"

"Because he would have lied just as straightforwardly on the other side. The others gave all the vices; Goodman would have given me all the virtues. You wanted unprejudiced testimony, of course. I knew you wouldn't get it from Goodman. I did believe you would get it from those others and possibly you did. But it was certainly less complimentary than I was expecting."

Mark Twain was making a hundred dollars a lecture and he thought he could afford to get married. He knew that Livy was used to the very best, but that was not the thing that would prevent their marriage. The truth was that Livy had been over-sheltered and overprotected all her life. Neither her mother or father wanted her to marry any man, let alone one who was known to use profanity and play cards for money. Moreover, Livy's father had boasted that so long as he was alive, no man would take her away from him. Jervis Langdon had changed his mind quite a bit since the day of that boast, but there were still obstacles before the pair could be married.

Mark got a loan of twelve thousand five hundred dollars from Livy's father to take a partnership in the Buffalo *Express,* but he still felt that he needed more financial security. Finally literature came to his rescue; *Innocents Abroad,* his sketches of the people who had made the trip on the *Quaker City,* sold so well that he could forget his financial worries. He was earning well over a thousand dollars a month from its amazing success, and over a hundred thousand copies of the book were sold the first year.

On February 2, 1870, Mark Twain, thirty-four, a prominent author, a rake who was presumably reformed (he was to fall again and again), and the happiest man in the world that day, married Olivia Langdon. The following day the whole Langdon family with friends took a special train to Buffalo. "I knew nothing about Buffalo," Mark Twain recalled in his *Autobiography,* "but I had made my household arrangements there through a friend, by letter. I had instructed him to find a boarding-house of as respectable a character as my light salary as editor would command. We were received at about nine o'clock at the station in Buffalo and were put into several sleighs and driven all over America, as it seemed to me— for apparently we turned all the corners in the town and followed all the streets there were—I scolding freely and characterizing that friend of mine in very uncomplimentary ways for securing a boarding-house that apparently had no definite locality. But there was a conspiracy—and my bride knew of it, but I was in ignorance. Her father, Jervis Langdon, had bought and furnished a new house for us in the fashionable street, Delaware Avenue, and had laid in a cook and housemaids and a brisk and electric young coachman, an Irishman, Patrick McAleer —and we were being driven all over that city in order that one sleighful of these people could have time to go to the house and see that the gas was lighted all over it and a hot supper prepared for the crowd. We arrived at last, and when I entered that fairy place my indignation reached high-water mark, and without any reserve I delivered my opinion to that friend of mine for being so stupid as to put us into a boarding-house whose terms would be far out of my reach. Then Mr. Langdon brought forward a very pretty box and opened it and took from it a deed of the house. So the comedy ended very pleasantly and we sat down to supper."

The new couple spent a happy winter, but then Livy's father died, and she was hard hit by the loss. In November, 1870, a son, Langdon, was born prematurely. The child was frail, and the two parents watched anxiously over him. As the months passed, the little boy's health improved, but he was never strong.

Mark and Livy left Hartford soon after the birth of their son. The *Express* had become a financial burden and the Clemenses did not find the society of Buffalo very congenial. Mark decided they would make their home in Hartford, Connecticut, which at that time was a publishing center and had attracted many writers.

Chapter *13*
Publishing

Mark worried about proving himself worthy of his wife, and his anxiety centered on the fact that he did not make enough money to support her in the style to which she was accustomed. He accepted another lecture series soon after they moved to Hartford, and was writing a book at the same time. He had put himself in the position of doing more than he should, of having to spread himself thin. He was editing a newspaper, writing books, and now he was going to lecture. Nevertheless, he insisted he could carry this heavy burden without hurting his artistic ability. He did not seem to understand that to produce great books, he needed time to reflect in peace and quiet. He needed to study and sort out the ideas that were whirling about in his head. He felt he could do many things at once, and often his writing suffered because of this.

But the paper was proving to take up too much time and giving too little in return. He sold his share, but at a loss. The male members of the Clemens family seemed to have inherited the poor business sense of their father. Orion was constantly in need of funds, and Mark sent him money. He was now convinced Orion would never hold a job which would support him.

Olivia tried to encourage his efforts in writing, but

she had little or no experience with artists and she did not always understand that Mark needed more time to contemplate than he was allowing himself. The two were never in conflict; they always thought alike, but they didn't always think in the best way for Mark Twain the writer. Both of them tended to be short-term thinkers.

In 1872, a girl, Susan, was born who was the opposite of Langdon in every way—strong, robust, healthy. Three months later the frail little boy died.

A few days before the boy's death, Mark had taken Langdon for a ride in the buggy. He was trying to use the time to sort out his chaotic thoughts. He fell into a deep reverie and when he came to himself, he saw that the blankets had slipped from his son's legs and that the boy was uncovered from the waist down, his bare legs exposed to the terrible cold. The next day Langdon had a high fever and the symptoms of a bad cold. Mark was sure that he had brought on the illness. All Mark's doubts and remorse from his childhood flooded back; he remembered how he had been a naughty boy and he thought of his carelessness then and of his irresponsibility now, for he held himself directly responsible for his son's death.

In the back of Mark Twain's mind there was always the fear that he did not deserve his good luck. He suspected that he would have to pay and pay and pay for his boyhood pranks, for the quick success of his writing, and for his great fortune in capturing Olivia Langdon. He still felt inferior to the cultured Easterners, and although he respected his own opinions and knew that he had a bright, quick mind, he also recognized that his formal education was scanty. He had read widely on his own but he had had to drop out of school when he was only eleven or twelve.

Underneath his humor and ready laughter was a deep and serious nature, one that questioned endlessly the workings of the universe. Why must man suffer as he does? Why did Langdon have to die? Why did he have to die so young and with his whole life ahead of him? Why did life so often seem to reward the bad and punish the good? What was the real nature of sin? These questions troubled Mark Twain all his life, and he tried to answer them honestly to himself and in his books. But he was careful never to preach, realizing that there is nothing people run from more than over-serious moralizing. He let his readers have fun with Huck and Jim as they drifted down the Mississippi, and he let them draw their own conclusions about the human worth of the slave, Jim, and about the deep relationship that developed between Huck and the Negro. This story was perhaps Mark Twain's best comment on the question of slavery.

In his new book, *Roughing It,* he gave a picture of life in the mining communities of the West as he had known it. He showed the trials and tribulations the emigrants and miners had gone through, and he described their grit and determination to better themselves. In this way, too, he showed the new spirit that was arising in America west of the Mississippi. The book was an enormous success. It won praise from the critics and it sold forty thousand copies in the first three months after it was published. Many things were passing through Mark Twain's mind in those three months. He grieved for his lost son but he rejoiced in his strong, healthy daughter. He also came to feel that writing was his life's work and that he must devote himself to it with all his energy.

All his life he was a warrier against injustice, and one battle which he got into at this time involved foreign copyright. A copyright is a method of insuring that an author receives money for his work. When a book is registered in the Office of Copyright in Washington, D.C., no unauthorized person may publish and sell the book.

Today books can be copyrighted in Europe as well as the United States, so that if a book is issued in a foreign country, the American author is protected and receives just payment. But at that time no such law existed. In Mark Twain's day a British publisher could "pirate" an American book, bring it out in England, and refuse to pay the author a cent. Mark felt this was a terrible injustice and he meant to stop it by going to England and finding an honest publisher who would bring out his books and promise to pay him his rightful royalties.

In August of that year Mark went to England to search out such a publisher. But he was concerned not only about his own work. He wanted to bring to the attention of the public the whole problem so that other authors might one day be protected, too.

He wrote many articles and spoke in public several times while he was in Britain. One of his last acts before returning home was to send a letter to the *Spectator,* a famous British publication, denouncing the stealing of American books by dishonest British publishers.

He returned home to find his wife radiant, his daughter, Susy, healthier and happier than ever. By now he was a famous person and people from both sides of the

Atlantic knew the name Mark Twain and respected it. Many people came to call, and there was a great deal of entertaining to be done. Their little house in Hartford was too small for large parties, so Mark decided to move to a larger place of his own design. Like everything else Mark Twain tackled, the new house was a direct expression of his strong, individual, outspoken personality. The Twains chose a site on Farmington Avenue. There were many trees and Mark Twain felt that the location was a lovely one. But the first plans submitted by the architect showed that the trees were to be cut to make room for the house. Mark Twain objected violently, and in the end the architect agreed to move the location of the house and save the trees.

Nor did Mark Twain want any of the conventional dark, cramped rooms so popular at the time. He wanted sunlight and a view of his trees and rooms with lots of space. People thought he was crazy to want such huge rooms with many windows, the sun streaming in, so many bathrooms, and—most of all—a billiard room on the third floor! But Mark Twain could relax over the billiard table; he got some of his best ideas there. He wanted to have one and he was going to have it, no matter what people said. He felt, too, that a man's home ought to be airy, sunny, and cheerful. Today we recognize that in house-planning, as in his writing, he was simply ahead of his time. His ideas are so accepted now that it seems strange to think that people laughed at him then and thought his notions were peculiar.

The Clemenses used to go every summer to Elmira to Quarry Farm, the house of Mrs. Crane, an adopted daughter of the Langdons. Mrs. Crane had named the

Reliving and writing about a glorious past

farm "Do-as-you-please Hall," and it was a fit name for the place. Here Mark Twain could do as he pleased— which to him meant settling down and getting a good deal of writing done. He was always happy at Quarry Farm because he was always working. It was here that Mark Twain began to relive in his mind his own childhood. It was here that he first conceived of Tom Sawyer and Huck Finn. It was here that he began to write down the adventures of these two boys which were to become world famous and which were to earn him a reputation as America's most beloved writer.

At Quarry Farm, in the summer of 1874 another girl, Clara, was born. In all the Twains had four children: one son, Langdon, who died at the age of twenty-two months, and three daughters, Susy, Clara, and Jean, who was born in 1880.

Now, too, Mark was supporting Orion and his mother, sending them a monthly check to make sure that they were provided for.

Many days during the summer months Mark sat in his study pondering his childhood. He remembered what life in Hannibal had been and what it had come to represent to him—the freedom and charm of boyhood, the essential democracy of the frontier people, and the openheartedness of his friends and family. He felt that the way of American life he had known as a boy was a unique one and one that had not been set down properly in literature. Mark Twain wanted to recapture that spirit; he wanted to tell people what life on the Mississippi was like, what the people thought and felt and dreamed. He began slowly and methodically to recapture all those old days and put them down on paper so that they would have a life of their own. For he understood that the event committed to the paper does have a life of its own. And that life lives long after the writer is dead.

He remembered the happy times at the Quarles farm and the old slave, Uncle Dan'l. He thought of his father's honesty and determination to repay debts he was not legally responsible for. He recalled his mother's vivacity, her love of animals, her loving concern for her children, her hatred of tyranny and her love of life itself.

He began to ask himself the big questions: What do I love in life? What do I hate in life?

And he thought he knew some of the answers. He loved a freedom of spirit and the kind of government which best expressed it—democracy. He loved the glamor and gaiety of life on the Mississippi in the fabulous days of the steamboats. He had loved swimming in Bear Creek and in the mighty river. He had loved exploring the limestone caves and going on Sunday school picnics. He had loved most the spirit of those boys who had gone off with a fishing pole over their shoulders, a wish in their hearts, and a whistle on their lips.

And he hated injustice and intolerance. He believed that no man should be intimidated by state or crown or church or caste. He thought that a man who was poor and exploited was a sad and sorry sight, a man whose spirit had been killed within him. And Mark Twain knew that more than anything else in life he valued the spirit of a free, independent man and he despised the things that killed that in him.

Always there came back to him the cry of the Mississippi: "M-a-r-k three! M-a-r-k three! Quarter-less-three! Half twain! Quarter twain! Quarter twain! *Mark twain!*"

The river had given him a whole way of thinking, the river had given him a name, the river had given him the legacy of his days as a steamboat pilot on its waters. He began to grow homesick for the old river. He had the first vague stirrings of an idea for another book, a book about piloting and about the river itself. That book was later to be called *Life on the Mississippi,* and it recounted all the stories of Mark's learning to be a pilot. But it went further than that. It gave an account of a whole way of life that had come to an end with the beginning of the Civil War. It told of the changes in the river, the river as it was now in the 1880s and as it had been during Mark's boyhood and adolescence. It was hard to believe the new Mississippi was the same as the one he had sailed so confidently with the *shape* of a river inside his head and with nothing else to guide him during the dark passages of the night. Now there were lights at the worst shoals and shallows, the dangerous points and turnings —lights that directed a pilot serenely through those troubled waters. And it was Horace Bixby that had designed those safety devices, the same Horace Bixby who had taught young Sam Clemens all he knew about the river. While writing *Life on the Mississippi,* Mark was constantly shifting between two people: the Sam Clemens who had been a cocky young river pilot and the Mark Twain who was now a married, settled man with an international reputation as a writer.

The trip back to the Mississippi set in his mind many adventures of the past which he thought he had forgotten. Now he was determined to finish his tale about Tom and Huck, and he came back to Quarry Farm and got to work on what were to be his two most famous books.

He had his troubles, however. Mark, like his father, had made bad investments, and he was often in need of money. He decided that he would go into the publishing business himself. That way, he would make money both as the author and as the publisher of his volumes.

In the year 1884 his Charles L. Webster Publishing Company was ready to start business. Its first book was *The Adventures of Huckleberry Finn.*

Much has been written in discussion of that book. It has been called one of the great American classics. It has been termed an anthology of humor, pathos, comedy, tragedy, social commentary, and political wisdom. It is probably all of these—and more. It *is* a great book and like any great book it deserves to be read more than it is discussed. Whatever else can be said for *The Adventures of Huckleberry Finn,* the finest thing that can be said of it is that every man, woman and child who can read ought to read it.

Another famous work that his publishing company brought out was the two-volume memoirs of General Ulysses S. Grant. General Grant had already finished two terms as President and had retired to private life. He put what little money had had into a banking house known as Grant and Ward. Two of the partners turned out to be scoundrels, carrying on enormous frauds. When the deception finally came to light, General Grant, who had been an innocent partner and whose name had persuaded many innocent people to put their money into the firm, was left absolutely penniless.

Grant needed to make a great deal of money. Although he was desperately ill with cancer of the throat, he embarked on the writing of his memoirs. In the winter of 1884 while Mark Twain was returning home from a lecture, he overheard two men talking. One was saying, "Do you know General Grant has actually determined to write his memoirs and publish them? He has said so to-day, in so many words."

The next morning Mark Twain went immediately to see the famous hero of Appomatox. General Grant and his son, Colonel Fred Grant, were in the library and they were looking over the contract for the book of memoirs. Grant was in the midst of signing; he actually had his pen raised to put his name to the paper when Mark Twain stopped him. "Don't sign it," he asked. "Let Colonel Fred read it to me first."

Mark Twain was shocked by the terms of the contract. The publisher had agreed only to pay Grant ten percent royalty. Twain insisted these terms were completely unfair. "Strike out the ten percent and put twenty in its place," he advised. "Better still, put seventy-five percent of the net returns in its place."

The General was astonished. The publisher would never agree to such terms, he insisted.

Twain argued, the General was immovable; finally Grant said that if Mark Twain was so certain he could get that much money for his memoirs, Twain could name the publisher who would pay it. Mark Twain said the General could sell the memoirs to him. He was a publisher.

Mark made the General an offer of a quarter of a million dollars, and finally persuaded Grant to leave the other publisher and come with his company. The general was desperately ill, but he worked on with all the spirit and determination he had shown in his campaigns against Lee. Grant wrote as many as ten thousand words at a sitting. Indeed, this final act of his life was perhaps the most heroic he ever performed. Just four days after he finished the last page of the manuscript, he died. But he had left his family well-provided for, and he had produced the means of settling his outstanding debts.

During the final visits of Mark Twain, Grant could not even speak. But he did live long enough to know that he had redeemed his honor. The whole country knew it as well. He was given a tremendous funeral and the heroic Grant received a hero's burial in a tomb on Riverside Drive in New York.

Huckleberry Finn and Grant's memoirs had been enormous successes, but there was still financial trouble for Mark Twain. He had become interested in a machine for setting type, remembering his old boyhood days at the Aments and all the time and trouble that he and the other men had had setting the type by hand. The typesetting machine would do away with setting type by hand, and Mark Twain was so sure that it would be a success that he had invested three thousand dollars on the patent. The inventor, J. W. Paige, worked on and on, but something was always the matter with the delicate mechanism. Parts would stop functioning, the machine would break down, there was constantly something that had to be fixed.

Year after year Mark Twain held onto his dream of an automatic typesetter just as his father before him had held onto the dream of the Tennessee land. And year after year he contributed more and more money to Paige. After five years of tinkering, Paige came to Hartford and told Mark Twain that the machine was almost ready. But there were still problems. He needed money. Mark Twain asked how much. Thirty thousand more will finish it, the inventor promised.

By 1888 the book publishing company was in difficulties. There had been disappointing books in which they invested a lot of money and which had poor sales. There were problems with the editors and directors, who were earnest but lacked knowledge and made costly mistakes.

The worry over finances and the increasing amount of money that Mark Twain was investing in the type-setting machine bothered him. He found that it was affecting his writing. When he sat down at the desk, all his worries overcame him, and he sat hour after hour staring at a blank piece of paper, unable to write. For a writer nothing could be more torturing, but he kept up a brave face, even when it was obvious to Livy that something was terribly wrong. She began economizing in every way possible, but still the income would not stretch to meet all of Mark Twain's commitments.

Finally he went to the place where he had always seemed to have inspiration, Quarry Farm, and here he finished *A Connecticut Yankee in King Arthur's Court*.

He was jubilant for a time, feeling that the book would be a best seller and would pull the publishing company out of its difficulties. It was the first Mark Twain book to be published in five years and the firm spent a good deal of money on publicity. But his hopes were dashed immediately after publication. Here was a book, the first book, that his critics did NOT like. Many of them did not understand it, and said that it lacked polish and taste. Others said that he had lost his knack of humor. Still others said the book was a bitter disappointment.

One thing is certain: it was a bitter disappointment to its author. Mark Twain had counted on *A Connecticut Yankee* to recoup the family fortune. He had invested a lot of money in publicity. He had banked all his hopes on a big sale. The sales were poor and the book showed no signs of picking up in popularity.

Things came swiftly to a head. Suddenly Mark Twain found that he owed a great deal of money and that there was no more money of his own to pay his debts. It was Livy who came to his rescue, insisting that he use her own fortune to get the family out of trouble. She paid sixty thousand dollars to Mark's creditors.

The family now seemed dogged by trouble. Olivia's mother and Mark Twain's mother died within a few months of each other. The typesetting machine was still in trouble and Paige needed more and more money. Desperate, Mark tried to find a group of businessmen who would help him with the financing of the machine, but none of them would touch it. It was a poor risk, they all said.

Now it became apparent that the Twains could no longer afford to keep up their lovely home. There was not enough money, no matter how much they cut corners. There seemed to be only one solution: they would have to shut up the house and go to Europe where it was cheaper to live.

In the summer of 1891 the whole family sailed for Europe. Mark was suffering from rheumatism, and they were desperately short of funds, but Livy tried to keep up their spirits.

The quiet of their life, away from all the friends and parties of Hartford, helped. Mark Twain began to write again, this time concentrating on a book called *Tom Sawyer Abroad,* on several articles and short stories, and on a book that he had had in his head ever since he was a child. This was to be the story of the French saint and martyr, Joan of Arc.

Back in Hannibal, when Mark was only thirteen years old, he had been walking down the street one day when a scrap of paper was blown to his feet. He picked up the paper and read it through. It was an account of some of the sufferings of the Maid of Orleans, and he was amazed and excited by what he read. Running home, he asked if the story were true. Told that it was, he determined then and there to find out everything he could about Joan.

For years he had studied the history of the saint who saved France, and now he began to write her life. In Florence, among the peace and beauty of the city, he felt that he could at long last understand and appreciate what had brought a humble girl to the notice of the God, and how God had spoken to her through the voices of St. Michael, St. Catherine, and St. Margaret. In those visions Joan had seen her role as savior of France.

The injustice of Joan's trial and execution, her great courage, and her strong belief in herself appealed to Mark Twain. He saw her as a great figure in the history of men and women who by their own fortitude had changed the course of history, and he determined to tell her story so that the world would never forget it.

Chapter 14

Disaster and Death

In 1893 one of the worst panics in the history of the United States occurred. Banks closed and never reopened, businesses failed, and some of the railroads even went bankrupt. Even though Mark Twain went back to New York, there was nothing he could do. He lost practically everything.

The publishing company was on the verge of bankruptcy. The typesetting machine was still not ready for use. Mark Twain could see no way out. Day after day he stayed in a small, cheap room overcome with the prospect of ruin. He did not know which way to turn. Every day new debts were piling up and he had no more money, no way of getting any more. He wanted to sell the publishing business, but the manager would not agree. Paige said his machine was soon to be in operating order, but even Mark Twain had by now lost faith in it.

For the first time in his life he felt completely defeated. He had been in trouble in 1891 when he had taken the family to Europe, but he had still believed in his ability to write books and make enough money to keep the publishing company going, to keep Paige supplied with necessary funds, and his family provided for.

It was true that the family had been living in reduced circumstances, but they had felt that this was only a temporary arrangement. They had kept their hope and optimism. Now there was nothing but debt and disaster ahead, and Mark Twain could not face returning to Europe and telling Livy and the children the facts. He had to force himself to go back, explaining as cautiously as he could. Olivia saw the truth immediately. The family moved to humble rooms in Munich and Mark returned to New York once more to see what he could do.

Then, at the worst moment of despair, an admirer came to his aid. H. H. Rogers, of the Standard Oil Company, heard from a friend of Mark Twain's plight, and came to offer his services. He took over the tangled finances of the writer and immediately began to make some sense out of them. He held hopes that the typesetting machine might be their salvation. He saw that the machine promised to save endless hours of labor and could greatly speed up the printing process. It was a delicate, contrary mechanism but *if* it could be made to work, Rogers felt that Mark would make a fortune. He renewed Mark's confidence in the invention and arranged to have a demonstration of its wonders in the *Times-Herald* building in Chicago.

Rogers had less hope of salvaging the publishing house, but he said he would do what he could. He started by selling the Library of American Literature, and saved the company from immediate bankruptcy. Mark Twain, encouraged, began to write again, free for a time from the worries which had nagged him. He finished *Pudd'nhead Wilson,* and wrote some short stories and articles. Feeling that he could now at last finish his book on Joan of Arc, he returned to Europe and his family to tell them the good news.

He had scarcely landed and started working in earnest when the Webster Publishing Company went bankrupt. The disaster which had been postponed and postponed was now a reality.

Rogers attempted to salvage what he could. He named Mrs. Clemens chief creditor, thereby saving Mark Twain's future royalties. If the creditors had claimed any royalties that Mark made in the future, the family would have been without any means of resources. The creditors received shares of the company, and Rogers told them a payment of fifty cents on the dollar would eventually be made. Rogers himself hoped, with Mark Twain, that the typesetting machine would save them. But in the end it proved hopelessly unreliable and had to be given up. There was now no other illusion that Mark Twain could hang onto. He knew then that he would have to write himself out of debt and disgrace, just as years before General Grant had done. If Grant had done it, ill as he was, he, Mark Twain, could do it.

Remembering his father, who had refused to turn his back on a debt of honor, remembering General Grant, who had redeemed his own honor, Mark Twain made his decision: the creditors would be paid in full, a full dollar for every dollar that was owed.

Rogers agreed. He said, "Business has its laws and customs and they are justified; but a literary man's reputation is his life; he can afford to be money poor but he cannot afford to be character poor; you must earn the cent per cent and pay it."

Later Mark Twain overheard Rogers and two other men talking.

"How old is Clemens?" the first man asked.

"Fifty-eight," Rogers replied.

"Ninety-five per cent of the men who fail at fifty-eight never get up again," the first man predicted.

"You can make it ninety-eight percent and be nearer right," the second said.

There were ninety-six creditors. Mark Twain was no longer young, and his decision to repay each of his creditors in full meant he would have to leave his family and go back to lecturing, where he had always made money. This time he would make a world tour.

Livy, seeing the depths of her husband's determination, decided to go with him. They spent two months at their beloved Quarry Farm getting ready for the departure. Susy and Jean were to be left behind, but Clara, then twenty-one, would accompany them. On July 15, 1895, Mark Twain, Olivia, and Clara started on a lecture tour around the world that would accumulate enough money to redeem the family honor.

The story of that fourteen months' tour is recorded in Mark Twain's book, *Following the Equator*. While he relates many of his adventures and tells of the countries he visited, he does not tell of the huge crowds that flocked to his lectures. He was making money and he was repaying his debts. He had given himself two years to pay off his creditors and now he was near the end of his obligations. In spite of his weariness he felt a sense of accomplishment.

It was a long, hard trip, but at the end of 1898 Rogers cabled the family in Vienna, "The creditors have all been paid a hundred cents on the dollar. There is eighteen thousand five hundred dollars left. What shall I do with it?"

Sailing to a new fortune

Mark Twain wired back, "Put it in Federal Steel." In two months he had a profit of a hundred and twenty-five per cent. He was free of financial worries at last.

Jean and Susy were to be reunited with the family in England, and all during the trip Livy and he had comforted themselves by saying, "When we get to England . . ." But when they got to England, neither of the girls was there to meet them. They found a letter instead saying that Susy had been taken ill. Frantic, they sent a wire to find out what was the matter. But Livy was so alarmed that she decided to leave with Clara the next day without waiting for an answer. The day that she left, Mark Twain received a cable that his favorite daughter had died.

"I was standing in our dining-room, thinking of nothing in particular," Mark Twain wrote in his *Autobiography,* "when a cablegram was put into my hand. It said, 'Susy was peacefully released to-day.'

"It is one of the mysteries of our nature that a man, all unprepared, can receive a thunder-stroke like that and live. There is but one reasonable explanation of it. The intellect is stunned by the shock and but gropingly gathers the meaning of the words. The power to realize their full import is mercifully wanting. The mind has a dumb sense of vast loss—that is all. It will take mind and memory months and possibly years to gather together the details and thus learn and know the whole extent of the loss."

Livy and Clara were on the high seas. There was no way to get the news to them. Mark Twain, in England, had to wait day after day imagining the two of them landing in America to receive that dreadful shock.

Mrs. Crane, Susy's aunt, was with her when she died. At the time when Livy and Clara had sailed for America, no one realized how ill Susy was. She had a sudden attack of meningitis and died three days later. She had been blinded by the disease and her last word has been "Mama," running her fingers over Mrs. Crane's face, and in her delirium believing that her mother had somehow got to her side.

For a time both Mark Twain and his wife gave way to despair. Not even the knowledge that they had paid all their debts could cheer them. Then Orion died, and Jean fell ill with a strange series of fits which was finally diagnosed as epilepsy.

Mark Twain felt that if he could just get his family back to Hartford, things might be better. He remembered how he and Livy had said, "When we get to London . . ." and he remembered the doctor's report from Sweden that Jean could not be cured. He saw the changes the past years had made in his wife—all the traveling on the lecture tour had exhausted her; then the news of Susy's death. Jean's illness had come on top of that—and he knew that he must face the fact that Livy was now almost completely an invalid. He felt old and tired and discouraged, but he tried to keep up his spirits for his beloved Livy. "When we get to Hartford . . ." he said again and again.

At the turn of the century the family started home. For the first time in months they began to act like themselves. They laughed and chattered, looking forward to seeing old friends, to being in the big, old house in Hartford, to being financially secure with the money from Mark's books.

True, things had changed drastically. Susy was gone, Susy whom they had loved with all their hearts. Livy was an invalid. Jean was ill. But . . . That word that he used to comfort his heart again and again: *But* . . .

Mark Twain's return to New York from his world tour was a hero's return. All the newspapers were full of his courage in repaying his debts. People everywhere praised and saluted him. His name was on everybody's lips. He was an American hero, an American hero come home to receive his honors.

The noise and excitement told on Livy. Mark finally realized that they could never go back to the big house in Hartford. It would simply be too much for his frail wife. They tried a summer in the Adirondacks, but Livy failed to rally. Finally the family found a house in River-dale-on-Hudson, and there they settled into a subdued but reasonably happy life. It could never be the old life, but now Mark Twain was realizing that nothing could ever bring back his past. But it was somewhere, even if he forgot it now and then: it was in his books, forever.

He was given honor after honor, including a degree from Yale University: the boy who had skipped school was now a "Doctor." He spoke often at banquets, and he was always being asked for articles and stories. But Livy was not responding as he had hoped, and finally, in 1903, he yielded to the advice of doctors and took her to Italy where he thought the warm sunshine might help her.

Ill as Livy was, Mark never lost hope. The villa in Florence to which the Twains went was damp and depressing, but Livy and Mark tried to keep up their spirits. One day she looked up at him and said, "You believe I shall get well?"

Mark Twain went cold. It was the first time in his life that he had ever heard his wife utter any kind of despair. He realized at that moment that she herself had given up hope of ever being well again.

He clung to the idea that if he could get Livy away from the damp villa where they were living she would improve. At last, after several months of searching, he found a place that he thought was perfect for an invalid. By this time Livy was so weak that he was only allowed to see her for fifteen minutes two or three times during a day, and he was bursting with the good news when he got home. "At seven that evening," he wrote, "I was at the bedside. I described the villa, exhibited its plans and said we would buy it to-morrow if she were willing, and move her to it as soon as she could bear the journey. She was pleased. She was satisfied. And her face—snow white, marble white, these latter weeks—was radiant."

During the afternoon of June 5, 1904, the villa had

a special warmth. Hope was in the air. Clara and Jean and Mark had felt as a fresh beginning were about to be made. Clara herself had said of her mother, "She is better to-day than she has been for three months," and Jean and her father agreed.

At seven Mark Twain went in to visit his wife. She was so bright and happy that he could not tear himself away from her, even though he knew that he was not supposed to make his visits long. And Livy herself was uplifted at the thought of the new home they would soon be in. She insisted on talking although talking had been strictly forbidden her because it taxed her strength too much. Instead of the usual fifteen minutes, Mark Twain spent a half an hour with his wife. Then, feeling guilty, he started to leave, saying that he had been carried away by her own high spirits and had forgotten the time. He was afraid that he had tired her. But she would not listen to his apologies.

"You will come back?" she asked, for at half-past nine every night he always came to say good-night.

Mark Twain went to his room, his heart bursting with happiness. For the first time in twenty-two months he felt that Livy *would* get better. Finally, so exhilarated by his own hopes for the future, he went to perform an act he had not done in years. In his own words, "I did a thing which I have hardly done since we lost our incomparable Susy eight years ago, whose death made a wound in her mother's heart which never healed—I went to the piano and sang the old songs, the quaint negro hymns which no one cared for when I sang them, except Susy and her mother. When I sang them Susy always came and listened; when she died, my interest in them

[161]

passed away; I could not put force and feeling into them without the inspiration of her approving presence. But now the force and feeling were all back, in full strength, and I was all alive, and it was as if eight years had fallen from me. In the midst of 'My Lord He call me! He call me by the thunder!' Jean crept into the room and sat down, to my astonishment and—embarrassment; and I stopped, but when she asked me to go on, only the astonishment remained, and it was a pleasant one and inspiring. With great difficulty I brought up little by little the forgotten words of many songs, and Jean remained until a servant came and called her out."

After a time Mark Twain stopped playing. It was near nine-thirty and time to say good-night to his wife. He was thinking to himself that he would tell Livy that Jean had come in to listen to the old spirituals. In his mind, he thought of the words he would use to his wife. "Livy, Jean has paid me a compliment which I have not had since we last—" Then he stopped in the middle of the thought. If he said that, he would remind Livy of Susy's death. There were so many things that could not be said these days.

But Livy had heard the singing. At a quarter past nine she had looked up and said to the nurse, "He is singing a good-night carol for me." The next moment, while he was on the stairs on his way up to bid her good-night, she died.

Chapter *15*

The Last Years

He left Europe and returned to America. He had ceased being the man he was: now he spent all his effort on the questions which rose in his consciousness, the old questions of the workings of the universe. Over and over he pondered the qualities of justice, the meaning of cruelty and injustice, the spirit that illuminated a man's life. He was forever asking himself what it was that was at the heart of a man, what it was that was man.

He lived for a time in New York, then moved to Connecticut where he had a large house constructed with —of course—a billiard room. Clara married the famous pianist and conductor, Ossip Gabrilowitsch, and moved away. He and Jean were left alone in the house.

For two years Jean's epilepsy forced her into a sanitarium. All the while Mark never gave up hope that one day she would be over her seizures. At the end of two years she was not cured, but she was well enough to come home. At the house the two of them began getting acquainted all over again. Now she was all the family Mark Twain had, and the two became very close. Jean would never marry. Clara was away with her husband. Livy and Susy were dead. Mr. Rogers died—"one of the best friends I ever had, and the nearest perfect, as man and gentleman, I have yet met among my race," Mark Twain wrote of him. The father and daughter clung together, determined to keep each other from bitter memories, determined to preserve the myth that two could fill all the gaps that the three missing members of the family had left.

In 1909 Mark Twain took a holiday trip to Bermuda for his health, leaving Jean in charge of the house with Kate Leary, the housekeeper who had been with the family nearly thirty years. Mark felt he could trust Jean in Kate's care, and the Bermuda vacation was a great success. He returned just before Christmas in high spirits. Jean was waiting for him on the dock, as were many newspaper reporters. Mark Twain was so famous now that whatever he did was news.

Jean was arranging a Christmas surprise for her father and she begged him not to peek into the loggia, where she had stored the gifts. The night he arrived home the two played cards, and Jean tried to teach him a new game she called "Mark Twain." When she left the room, he couldn't help stealing a look where the presents were concealed. "The loggia floor was clothed with rugs and furnished with chairs and sofas; and the uncompleted surprise was there: in the form of a Christmas tree," he remembered, "that was drenched with a silver film in a most wonderful way; and on a table was a prodigal profusion of bright things which she was going to hang . . ."

The day before Christmas Eve Jean and her father were very close. They had a festive dinner, Jean laughing and chatting about the coming Christmas surprise, never guessing that her father had "cheated" and looked.

The two strolled from the dinner table hand in hand and went into the library where they continued their conversation until nine, so happy to be with one another after their absence that they did not want to break apart, even though Jean had last minute Christmas preparations to finish.

Mark told his daughter that he had never seen her look as well or the house in such splendid order. He felt that she was almost well and that if she continued in such good spirits, he might return to Bermuda in February. Jean said if he would wait another month she would go with him. They shook hands, sealing the bargain.

Finally, reluctantly, Jean got up, her dog following her to the door. To Mark Twain he looked like a wolf, but the animal was gentle and kind and followed Jean everywhere. The dog had been raised in Germany and could understand no English. Jean, who was good at languages, always spoke to him in German. Now she said something softly to the dog. Then, turning to her father, she said, "I can't kiss you good night, father: I have a cold and you could catch it."

Mark Twain bent and kissed her hand.

Impulsively, moved by his gesture of affection, she seized his hand and kissed it in return. "Sleep well, dear!" she cried, and went to her room.

Jean had the habit of leaving the house around seven-thirty in the morning and riding horseback to the station for the mail. When she returned, she sorted the mail and worked on those letters that she answered for her father. She was a conscientious secretary, even fishing letters out of the wastepaper to answer. She said that if people cared enough to write they deserved an answer.

When she had finished her correspondence, she again rode back to town to post the mail, then she spent the day supervising the farm. Sometimes, in the evening, she would play billiards with her father. In spite of her malady, she was active and energetic.

At half past seven the morning of Christmas Eve, Mark Twain awoke to the sound of voices in the hall. He thought it was Jean, setting out for the mail. He smiled to himself, happy to be home for Christmas. He heard the door open and said to himself that Jean was going to come in to kiss him good morning. No one else, he knew, would enter without knocking.

Kate Leary, the housekeeper, stood in the doorway. She was white and shaking. *"Miss Jean is dead!"* she cried.

Jean had had a convulsion in her bath, followed by a heart attack. She had died without a cry.

All that day Mark Twain wandered about the house, one phrase in his mind: *Jean is dead!* The dog, too, seemed to know what had happened; he slunk about lost and dismayed. In the middle of the day Mark Twain went again to see the Christmas decorations that Jean had been working on. "Such a turmoil of Christmas presents for servants and friends!" he wrote in the last chapter of his *Autobiography*. "They are everywhere; tables, chairs, sofas, the floor—everything is occupied and over-occupied. It is many and many a year since I have seen the like. In that ancient day Mrs. Clemens and I used to slip softly into the nursery at midnight on Christmas Eve and look the array of presents over. The children were little then. And now here is Jean's parlor looking just as that nursery used to look. The presents are not labeled— the hands are forever idle that would have labeled them today. Jean's mother always worked herself down with her Christmas preparations. Jean did the same yesterday and the preceding days, and the fatigue has cost her her life. The fatigue caused the convulsion that attacked her this morning. She had had no attack for months . . . .

". . . on her desk a long list of names—fifty, he thinks—people to whom she sent presents last night. Apparently she forgot no one. And Katy found there a roll of banknotes for the servants."

Mark Twain could not bring himself to go back to the old house for the funeral. He said his goodbyes to Jean in this last house where they had been so close. The hearse drew up on Christmas night at six to take away his daughter. Mark Twain's, biographer, A. B. Paine, was there playing several numbers that Mark Twain request- ed—Schubert's *Impromptu*, Jean's favorite; *Intermezzo*, for Susy; the Handel *Largo*, for Olivia.

Snow was falling. Mark Twain stood at the window and watched the hearse drive away. She was going to her childhood home where she would be buried by her mother's side, next to Susy and Langdon.

On December 26th he wrote the last entry that was to appear in his *Autobiography*, sealed it and mailed it to Paine, with instructions to use it if Paine thought it fitting. The words that Mark Twain wrote were:

"*2:30 P.M.*—It is the time appointed. The funeral has begun. Four hundred miles away, but I can see it all just as if I were there. The scene is the library in the Langdon homestead. Jean's coffin stands where her mother and I stood, forty years ago, and were married; and where Susy's coffin stood thirteen years ago; where her mother's stood five years and a half ago; and where mine will stand, after a little time.

"*Five o'clock.*—It is all over.

"When Clara went away two weeks ago to live in Europe, it was hard but I could bear it, for I had Jean left. I said *we* would be a family. We said we would be close comrades and happy—just we two. That fair dream was in my mind when Jean met me at the steamer last Monday; it was in my mind when she received me at the door last Tuesday evening. We were together; *we were a family!* the dream had come true—oh, preciously true, contentedly true, satisfyingly true! and remained true two whole days.

"And now? Now Jean is in her grave!

"In the grave—if I can believe it. God rest her sweet spirit!"

Those were the last words that Mark Twain wrote for publication; four months later, on April 21, 1910, Mark Twain finished the last chapter of his life.

The man was dead; now the legend began to live.

Chapter 16

Mark Twain the Man

How does a man become a legend?

The legendary man is the one whose personality stamps its mark indelibly on the minds of his own generation and the generations that follow him. Great warriors, statesmen, explorers, inventors, scientists, visionaries, artists—men who in some way alter the world by their work or deeds—become legends. Sometimes a man has such a dazzling personality that a whole body of anecdotes are attached to his name, and he lives on as a legend in the minds of other men.

Of all the men in the history of American literature, Mark Twain remains the best-known and the best-loved —both as a man and as a writer. He has become a living legend—a legendary personality and a legend as a writer.

First of all, he had a striking, memorable appearance. His huge head of auburn hair, his big curling auburn mustache and his bright, dancing eyes caught the public's imagination. His conversation from early adolescence impressed everyone, particularly his slow, drawling accent—what his mother called "Sammy's long talk."

When he was older, his hair turned completely white, and Mark Twain emphasized his picturesque white walrus mustache and his lionlike mane of white hair by dressing in white suits. It is little wonder that he commanded attention wherever he went.

People who came to see him out of curiosity, however, stayed to respect his wit and humor, for he was a superb talker. Early in life he had learned how to tell a good story—first as a pilot on the Mississippi, later as a miner around the campfires of the West. He was a part of the story-telling tradition that the pioneers perfected. People always remarked over his fabulous fund of stories. They remembered how he roamed about as he talked, his hands clasped behind his back, his voice charming everyone with its soft, Missouri accent. Often, at dinner parties in his own home, he would get up between courses and stroll up and down, discussing and discoursing, while the guests paused over their food, fascinated by his wit, his wisdom, and his epigrams.

His was a personality that always attracted people. He seemed to have been born with a limitless amount of charm. He had come in with the appearance of Halley's comet in 1835 and, in later years, he used to tease his biographer and friends by remarking that anyone who came in with a comet was destined from the start to make a name for himself. He used to say that since he had come in with the comet, he would go out with it—and he did. As he lay dying, Halley's comet once more flashed across the sky.

That the heavens seemed to conspire with his own flamboyance does not seem far-fetched. He was always in the thick of excitement. He was always where new things were happening, where people were trying to create a new kind of world. He was forever the spectacular personality doing unusual or outrageous things.

Secondly, more than any one man in his century, Mark Twain came to symbolize an era. He had done all the things that made the nineteenth century exciting and vital. He had been born at the gateway to the frontier, in almost the center of a nation that was just beginning to come into its own. He had grown up on the banks of America's greatest river. He had been a pilot on its treacherous waters. He had worked for little village newspapers whose humor and insights formed the image of the West. He had prospected for silver. He wrote books that extolled the life of the new West, that praised the pioneers and their children who were making a new nation in space and in spirit. He had gone across the Pacific and across the Atlantic to see with the eyes of a frontiersman worlds that were unlike his own. He had written of America as no other writer before or after him, putting the essence of the American spirit into his books and the excitement of the American dream into his characters.

In many ways he carried with him the legacy of new life that people life Judge and Jane Clemens had gone to find. His father represented the genteel aristocracy of a settled part of the nation, Virginia; his mother had that vital spark of life that frontier families needed in order to survive. Sam Clemens was both his mother's and father's child. From his mother he got much of his charm—his peculiar way of speaking, his forthright attitude toward life, his hatred of injustice and cruelty, his love of life itself. From his father he inherited the grit and determination to make the most of his life, to uphold the honor and values of an enlightened man.

Sam Clemens grew up in a house where the love of

intangible values—honoring one's word, meeting one's debts, standing by one's vows—was strong. The Clemens household was built on the dual code of fighting against wrong and fighting for right.

Hannibal, Missouri, the town in which he grew up, opened on the great expanse of the West. By its main street the mightiest river in America flowed—a river thronged with endless legends of men and deeds. The boys of Hannibal were familiar with the strong acts of courage of the pioneers. They knew all the folk tales of the fabulous men who had opened up the West. Their whole lives were colored by a respect and admiration for the brave, strong, courageous man who stood against all odds for the things in which he believed.

Mark Twain loved the surrounding countryside with its big cottonwood trees, its meandering creeks, its simple pleasures. He was always alert to the mysteries and beauties of nature. But he was aware, too, of the violence that lurked behind the peaceful exterior. Mark never forgot the two boys who had drowned, he never forgot the tramp who was burned alive in the town jail, he never forgot the corpse lying in the moonlight on the floor of his father's office.

He had loved the Quarles farm, and he remembered the slaves there who had taught him so much. He carried with him the sound of Sandy's singing in his own house. He remembered the slaves who were sold down river. He kept vivid in his mind the brutality he had once witnessed against a slave. Slavery for a boy growing up in the South was a source of dual emotions. Young Sam Clemens played with little Negro boys. He felt a companionship with the Negro men that he did not feel with his own father. He knew and loved and respected many slaves, and as he grew older the evil of slavery was always on his mind. He came to see it as a blot on the national integrity, an evil which would not simply be undone by the Emancipation Proclamation. No, the evil of slavery would be with the new nation for a long time to come.

The slaves taught the young boy much. He heard stories that no white men ever told, for the slaves had a treasury of stories all their own. He listened to their superstitions and fears, and he absorbed their feelings about religion. Above all, he loved the Negro spirituals, which became so deeply a part of his life. It was the music of the river, his river, the Mississippi.

Wherever he went Mark Twain carried Hannibal, the Quarles farm, and the river with him. Now they are forever imprinted in his books, a part of literary life.

When Horace Bixby taught his young cub to know the *shape* of the Mississippi river, he was also teaching him how to impress on his mind details—the small things that reveal so much about the large one. Mark Twain's books were immeasurably enriched by this training. When he had to use all his mental resources to learn the Mississippi, he was developing his powers of observation to a high pitch. Ever after this would be invaluable to him as an artist.

His life on the Mississippi did much to form his thinking. During his days as a pilot on the mighty river, he evolved his philosophy of life. He wrote in his notebook: "Take it [life] just as though it was—as it is—an earnest, vital and important affair. Take it as though . . . the world had waited for your coming. Take it as though it was a grand opportunity to do and achieve . . ."

He followed that youthful advice to himself all his life. His outlook was one of the optimist. True, there were terrible moments of doubt—the deaths of Henry, his brother; Langdon, his son; Susy and Jean, his daughters; Livy, his wife—which made him question the workings and meaning of life. But he never for long gave up hope that a better world was around the corner. Even in the depths of despair, his humor never deserted him.

With the outbreak of the Civil War, he was to leave the river and take part in one of the worst experiences of a man's life. Although Mark Twain did not serve longer than a few weeks, he remained until the end of his life struck with the horror of the one death for which he held himself at least partially responsible. "I would have given anything then—my own life freely—" he wrote of the stranger he and the others killed, "to make him again what he had been five minutes before . . . the taking of that unoffending life seemed such a wanton thing. And it seemed an epitome of war; that all war must be just that—the killing of strangers against whom you feel no personal animosity. . ."

Sickened by that unnecessary killing, he left the Confederate militia. It is little wonder he headed West. The violent energy of America was in him, and there was no other real choice for him but to move West, to join the men who had gone out to Nevada to seek their fortunes in silver. He went by stagecoach. He saw the Pony Express. He lived and worked in the silver mines. He was seeing America in the making.

It was the uncommon common man who went West, the man who was not afraid to face the unknown, the man who was looking for something in the new areas that he had not found in the settled ones. Many of these men were not quite sure what they were looking for, but it was basically for a new way of life. In part, of course, there was the promise of riches—gold or silver or land. But it was much more than material riches that those men sought. The people in the wagon trains and the prospectors had a vision of the New Community where a man would be judged by his own qualities, and not by birth or wealth or social position.

Mark Twain proved that the dream of the West was possible. He was a poor boy from a backwoods community who rose to the top of his profession. His talent and his will power took him to that high place, not influence or contacts or inheritance.

No matter what the adventure on which he embarked, Mark Twain was always conscious of the power of the pen. Even, happy as he had been on the river in his pilot days, he wrote. In the mining period he wrote sketches and sent them to the *Territorial Enterprise*. He had printing ink in his veins. It is little wonder that in the end he came to his real calling: that of the writer.

He remained the restless Westerner, even when he was writing. He travelled to San Francisco and met other writers, important writers like Bret Harte, the author of "The Luck of Roaring Camp" and many other famous stories of the West; Artemus Ward, author of a humorous column called "Artemus Ward's Sayings," which used misspellings, odd situation, and the unusual Western attitude to achieve its humor; and Charles Warren Stoodard and Orpheus C. Kerr. These men talked with Mark Twain. They met and discussed their problems in writ-

Yarn spinning with Bret Harte

ing. They helped each other establish the new literature that was growing up around Western life.

Mark Twain went to the Hawaiian Islands and tramped everywhere, seeing things at first-hand, and jotting down his vivid impressions.

"The Celebrated Jumping Frog" had given him his first taste of national acclaim. His account of the sinking of the *Hornet* and the terrible hardships of the survivors was published across the country and greatly increased his fame. "Sammy's long talk" had always impressed everyone, and it was natural that he should eventually turn to lecturing as one more field to conquer.

He was a splendid lecturer, holding his audiences spell-bound. He had a way of pausing to emphasize key words, of lazily building up to his point. Seemingly he was taking his time, but in reality he was piling climax upon climax until at last he brought the house down with a laugh that rolled over the stage in a great crescendo.

His was the Western style of telling an anecdote. Through every one of his absurd exaggerations, he kept a poker face. With all his wild tales and uproariously funny lines, he never betrayed any emotion. His lecturing was an important contribution to the growing legend of Mark Twain the man, for it brought his name before the public more than the name of any other author.

In addition to his writing and lecturing abilities, he had a number of other accomplishments—he was a moving singer, particularly of the Negro spirituals he loved; he could play the guitar well and the piano better than average. But the outstanding thing about him, everyone who knew him agreed, was the quality of his speaking voice, which was beautiful, expressive, and capable of infinite varieties of expression.

By the time he was forty his name was a household word. People knew who Mark Twain was, and in every club and parlor over the country his latest observations and jokes were passed along.

His restless temperament—the restless spirit of the West—never left him. He could not stay in one place long, not even a place where he had made himself famous. He left America for a trip to Europe and the Holy Land, saying that he wanted to "suggest to the reader how *he* would be likely to see Europe and the East if he looked at them with his own eyes instead of the eyes of those who traveled . . . before him." In that statement stands Mark Twain's code. He wanted to look with *fresh* eyes. He would not accept the evaluations of the past.

But there was another American spirit in the trip of the *Quaker City*. The purpose of the trip was to provide the passengers with culture as well as entertainment. America was beginning to feel its lack of a historic past. It was beginning to be embarrassed by the raw newness of the nation. Now that the material wealth of the country had provided the means to travel, the middle-classes were beginning to want to see Europe for themselves. Formerly only the wealthy could afford to go abroad. In Mark Twain's day many families were enjoying the privileges and pleasures once reserved for the rich.

Many of these people had little or no cultural background. They had not been well-educated. They had made their money recently. But they felt themselves as good—or better—than their old-established rich Eastern "neighbors." Now they were going to see Europe for themselves. To them Europe was a kind of glass showcase full of wonders of the past to be oohed and ahed over. They thought of Europe as "quaint." While they admired the works of art, the cathedrals and museums, the palaces and castles, they felt too that culture was not an excuse for poor plumbing and cold houses. Mark's book tells of their attitude, which to some extent he shared—their horror at the inequality among people, their scorn at the privileges of the nobility, their disgust at the tyranny of the church. To Mark and to many others, much of Europe was not only a showcase of old masters, it was also a showcase of poverty, ignorance, exploitation, corruption, and conservatism, and he did not hesitate to say so.

He couldn't tolerate the "stuffed shirts"—real Westerner that he was—and he hated the terrible poverty he saw. He felt that all men deserved a decent place to live, decent clothes and adequate food. But he did not shut his eyes to the short-comings of his fellow-travellers. He knew they often behaved badly and he despised their habit of cutting their initials on famous relics, of carting off souvenirs, and of talking in loud voices about the relative merits of Europe and America. To most of the pilgrims there was absolutely no comparison at all: America was the biggest, best place in the world.

He came back of America and married. For a time it seemed he would settle down. He built a beautiful—if strange—home in Hartford. He learned to know all the "literary lights" in Boston and New York. He made a special friend of William Dean Howells, a famous critic and novelist. Howells—a cultivated Easterner—was enormously respected, and he had a great deal of influence on Mark Twain.

But even Howell's restraining influence could not stem the speculator in Mark Twain. To the end he was a Westerner seeing a new fortune around the corner. Mark Twain had no more business going into the publishing field than he did investing in a typesetting machine. He had no head for business and he wouldn't admit this limitation. Of course he could sell books! Of course he could get a machine that would do away with setting type by hand! But he forgot that you cannot run a publishing house on the theory that you will put out one best seller after another. Publishing houses must have books that sell reasonably well year after year; they cannot depend on a few spectacular successes. Typesetting machines must be workable at a moderate cost; it doesn't make any difference how marvelous a machine is, it must work more than it breaks down; it must be reasonable to run. Otherwise it is an oddity, nothing more.

But Mark Twain was always the man from the West who would stake his fortune on a lucky turn of the wheel or a sudden strike in silver. In the early 1880s he tried to patent a steam generator which cost him a fortune. Then he invested thirty-two thousand dollars in a steam pulley. Next he invested in a watch company, an insurance company, a chalk-plate process, and lost somewhere near fifty thousand dollars. He had a chance to invest in the telephone, but turned that down, saying that he didn't want "anything more to do with wildcat speculation." How little he knew himself. The wildcat speculation in the typesetting machine was to eat up his fortune and to set him to wandering again. It is said he invested three hundred thousand dollars in Paige's typesetting machine!

In his later life he lived in London, Vienna, Paris, Berlin, Italy, Switzerland, and Sweden as well as in the United States. Even in Europe his personality attracted visitors, and the family would no sooner settle down than a procession of guests would be at the door, anxious to partake of that famous talk that some said was more representative of his genuis than his writing was. Once his daughter Jean remarked, "Why, papa, if it keeps on like this, pretty soon there won't be anybody for you to get acquainted with but God."

Nevertheless, all the adulation never turned his head. He retained his humility, his knack of holding on to the common touch. He still judged men by what they were, not by their rank or position or money. He served at the age of seventy as pallbearer for his coachman, saying that the man was his ideal of the perfect gentleman.

He had a few eccentricities, like all unusual personalities. In later years these quirks became more pronounced. His love of billiards amounted to an obsession. He said that he thought he walked at least ten miles a day around a billard table. And it was not unusual for him to play all night when the urge struck him. He had a hatred for noises, and any small consistent noise—the ticking of a clock, the rattling of paper, someone whistling tunelessly—could drive him to distraction. He was a showy dresser and he became a conspicuous actor when he felt the center of attention was drifting away from him.

In other words, he did not disdain adulation. Legends never do.

It has been said that his personality was more striking in the history of American literature than his writing. There is certainly no doubt that his vitality and his vivid language made him memorable not only in his own time but remained after death to cast a spell over future generations.

Chapter **17**

Mark Twain the Writer

Mark Twain's achievement, in spite of his fabulous personality, rests upon his books. One day people will no longer remember the man in the white suit with the big mustache and the shock of white hair, but people will still read *Tom Sawyer, The Adventures of Huckleberry Finn, The Prince and the Pauper, A Connecticut Yankee in King Arthur's Court,* and *Life on the Mississippi.*

Huck and Tom live as no other two boys in all of fiction. Tom is the eternal boy bound and wound up in adventure. Tom is the dreamer on the banks of the Mississippi, seeing all the excitement of the world in its waters, feeling that the great waterway is the road to freedom. The river brings all kinds of people and experiences to Tom Sawyer's sleepy little town of St. Petersburg (in reality Hannibal); it permits a boy to escape the monotony of his life and find adventure and excitement on its shores and islands. On the Mississippi Tom Sawyer gets, as Mark Twain said of himself, "secrets not to be got out of books, but only acquirable by experience."

Huck's river is different from Tom's. Huck's Mississippi is the river of a boy growing up and understanding new things, seeing the world in a new way. Just as the life around Huck was growing up and coming of age, so does Huck himself come of age in the book.

Tom sees only the good in the river, but Huckleberry Finn accepts good and evil as living side by side. He knows both the dreamy, romantic quality of the river and also the horror and supersition and violence that are a part of it. Tom and Huck themselves are representative of two kinds of life, of two kinds of attitude. Tom is the young boy, the schemer, the prankster, the romantic. Tom has a home and love. He uses the river as a means to fulfill all the dreams of adventure that the average young boy has.

But Huck is a realist. He does not look at the world through rose-colored glasses as Tom does. He has had a hard life. His mother is dead. His father is the town drunkard. He must shift for himself. He has learned that life is not easy. Tom is protected. Huck is not.

Therefore, Huck must find a code all his own. He must go further into life than Tom. He must judge things for himself. He cannot use what people have told him because very few people bother to tell him anything. While Tom is sure he is always right, because he knows what people should do, Huck is full of doubts. He knows what people tell him he ought to do, but he can never be sure people are right. His own eyes often show him that people say one thing and do another. He has to find out what is right for himself.

Huck, then, becomes the true free boy in search of real meaning in his life. He listens to his own heart, he makes up his own mind, he does not carry the common prejudices of the people with him.

Huck's real development comes in relation to "Nigger Jim." He respects Jim and loves him because he sees Jim's fine nature, just as on the Quarles farm Mark

Twain had loved and admired Uncle Dan'l.

Of course the reader *wants* Huck to help Jim. The reader sees that Huck is right. His idea of respect for a man, regardless of the color of his skin, is more advanced than the things he has been taught. In this way Mark Twain expressed his feelings about slavery more forcefully than all the preaching in the world could do. The law of slavery was wrong. Jim runs away to escape those laws. So does Huck. They take to the river in the search for their freedom, and the river teaches them each something new: on the Mississippi a man is a man regardless of the color of his skin.

This lesson is further spelled out in Mark Twain's book *Pudd'nhead Wilson.* "Why were niggers *and* whites made? What crime did the uncreated first nigger commit that the curse of birth was decreed for him? And why is this awful difference made between white and black?" Mark Twain makes one of his characters ask.

In the society of the time, there was no way to escape the terrible penalty of being born black. But on the river —the free river—that crime no longer existed. The Mississippi—"a whole mile broad," as Huck says, "and awful still and grand"—is the real hero of Huckleberry Finn. The river knows no law save itself. It is the river of Mark Twain as he knew it best: a testing place for men.

He was to write of it often. His fullest picture occurs in *Life on the Mississippi,* where he describes in detail the days he spent as a cub under Horace Bixby and his life as a river pilot. But *Life on the Mississippi* is much more than this. It is a rounded picture of all shades of life along the Mississippi. There are the sleepy, little villages like Hannibal, where he grew up. There is the float-

The true hero. . "awful still and awful grand"

ing world of the steamboat. There are the frontier fail-
ures, the squatters who live in meanness and poverty. For
the frontier could punish a man cruelly, rob him of
his courage and defeat his dreams, as well as it could reward another man with fabulous riches. Men like Mark
Twain's father came to know the bitterness of poverty
and the disillusionment of their dreams. They turned in-
ward—quiet, defeated men who, as Thoreau had said
earlier, lived lives of quiet desperation.

Still men like Mark's father held on to their honor.
But the poor whites living along the river were bitter.
They had come West to find a new life and they had
found only the old one: poverty and ignorance, injustice
and violence.

But Mark Twin loved them all. He saw their failings
and he understood their ways. He wrote of them as he
saw them, and he filled *Life on the Mississippi* with all

their portraits. He had a special admiration for the courageous, self-reliant, strong, brash bargemen. To him they symbolized the strength even the lowest of the men had. But he did not sentimentalize them. He saw also their coarseness and brutality. But they produced heroes—men of enormous strength and unheard-of courage. He liked to listen to their tall stories and jot down their dialect. They grounded him in the savage humor of the West.

It was Nevada, of course, that was the real West. And Mark Twain was meant to write a book about that, too. *Roughing It* tells his experiences in the mining camps. This book tells the stories of the overland coachmen, the pony express riders, the men who went prospecting. It tells of a land that made giants and broke the weak, and of the colorful times that will never come again.

Virginia City, with its towering mountain above it, seemed a symbol of the height to which the lowest man could ascend. In America a man need not remain poor and powerless. With hard work and determination he might be able to carve out fabulous successes for himself. Yet as Mark Twain matured, he also realized that material wealth alone was not enough. There had to be spiritual growth as well. His later books point to this—*The Prince and the Pauper, A Connecticut Yankee in King Arthur's Court, Joan of Arc, The Gilded Age.*

In Nevada Mark Twain was at the crossroads of his life. He had come to the point of giving up the dream of easy riches. He now knew that he would spend the rest of his life writing. His problem was to equip himself to write in the best way possible. He did not want to write fancy "literary" pieces. He wanted the air of the West in his books. He wanted the talk of Westerners to come from the mouths of his characters.

Joe Goodman, who ran the Virginia City newspaper, gave him some of the best advice of his life. Mark Twain had not been with the paper long when Goodman said, "Never say we learn so and so, or it is rumored, or we understand so and so; but go to headquarters and get the absolute facts; then speak out and say it *is* so and so. In the one case you are likely to be shot, and in the other you are pretty sure to be; but you will preserve the public confidence."

That kind of honesty marked the writing of Mark Twain all his life. He never thought so and so, or took someone else's word for so and so. He went out and saw for himself and said it *is* so and so.

As Goodman had predicted, that honesty was often to get him in trouble, but he did win the public's confidence. After he had been writing only a short time for the *Territorial Enterprise,* the Virginia City legislature feared his pen. It could ridicule a man and make him the laughing stock of the town. Mark Twain became the most adept political writer in the territory. Mark himself said, "I was a newspaper reporter four years in cities, and so saw the inside of many things; and was reporter in a legislature two sessions and the same in Congress one session, and thus learned to know personally three sample bodies of the smallest minds and the selfishest souls and the cowardliest hearts that God makes."

It was strong language. He always called a spade a spade. He said exactly what he thought while he was in Nevada, he said exactly what he thought in Europe. His book, *Innocents Abroad,* is full of his forthright, honest opinions. For that reason it is much more than just a travel book. It is a record of a man seeing a new kind of world and making up his mind what is valuable and what is not. To make up his mind Mark Twain had often to call in question many things that he had taken for granted. In searching his own conscience, he makes others search theirs.

At one period during his life he and Charles Dudley Warner wrote a book together which criticized the corruption of the life of that time. The book was called *The Gilded Age,* and much of the writing which Mark Twain contributed to it was the result of his observations as a newspaperman, lecturer, traveler, and student of human nature. The book is an uneven one. This is natural since two men took turns writing it. But it still has the imprint of Mark Twain. In *The Gilded Age* Mark Twain used members of his own family as models: Washington Hawkins was something of a portrait of himself, Lafayette was Orion; Colonel Sellers, one of his most famous character creations, was a portrait of a cousin, James Lampton.

There is an echo in *The Gilded Age* of the old Clemens failing of looking for riches in impossible places. The book is also a criticism of the newly rich who do not deserve their luck, and of the men who dream of mad schemes of making money without knowing how to carry them out. Certainly Mark Twain must have been remembering his own father when Squire Hawkins dies murmuring, "Never lose sight of the Tennessee land! . . . wealth that is boundless!" And there is little doubt that he thought of Orion when he had Washington Hawkins, old and shattered at thirty, curse that land. Washington says of the land that "it has cursed every hour of my life . . . We might all have been prosperous now; we might all have been happy, all these heartbreaking years, if we had . . . gone contentedly to work and built up our own wealth by our own toil and sweat . . . . Instead of that, we have suffered more than the damned themselves suffer!"

As Mark Twain grew older, he saw that human error was inevitable, but he also came to feel that it might serve as a means of refining the spirit. Through pain and suffering would come learning; through learning, refinement of the soul.

In *A Connecticut Yankee in King Arthur's Court*, Mark Twain contrasted his own times with the year 528. The hero of the book is "The Boss," a mechanic who is hit on the head and wakes up in the sixth century. He comes to the court of King Arthur and is horrified by all the ignorance and abuses he sees. He is particularly opposed to Merlin the Magician because he feels that Merlin is a superstitious humbug who is hoodwinking the people. The Boss is certain that all he has to do is apply the know-how of the late nineteenth century to the evils of King Arthur's Court and he will abolish all abuses.

The Boss in a way is Tom Sawyer grown up, but he is also Huck. He has the show-off-ness of Tom, combined with the shrewdness and ingenuity of Huck. He is boundlessly optimistic, sure that a machine can solve any problem. He is brash and bountiful and endlessly running about trying to patch up problems. But he is limited. The Boss does not recognize that technical advancements will not alone remake man. There has to be spiritual change as well.

Man must mature within as well as without. The Boss never stops trying to undo what he thinks is wrong, but he can only undo wrong with a new machine. He is blinded by his own limitations. In the end it is the superstitious Merlin who triumphs. Mark Twain is here proclaiming his idea that one man alone, even with all the machines in the world, cannot make society better. A dictator may be able to improve material conditions, but he lessens the spiritual values of all around him.

In *The Prince and the Pauper,* two boys exchange clothes and thereby exchange lives. The prince becomes the pauper, the pauper the prince. Both learn heartbreaking lessons. The real king is horrified by the life of the poor. The pauper is bewildered and upset by the ways of the rich. Mark Twain was trying to show in this book that absolute monarchy can paralyze the feelings of both big and little men. Such a system does not let men think for themselves. It does not let them judge men on their own merits. At the end, with the real king restored to his throne, there is some hope that he will improve conditions once he understands democracy.

The skeptical Yankee, Mark Twain, had used a fictional pair of boys to show his own hatred of pretention, bogus values, rank and nobility. He was once again looking at the world with the clear eyes that had memorized the shape of the Mississippi. He was seeing the world with the Westerner's sense of humor. He was writing with all the sharp sarcasm of the New World's insistence that a man is only what he proves himself to be by his own deeds.

"Sammy's long talk" was not meant just to amuse his friends and audiences. It went into his books as well. To teach was one thing, but it was not enough. Mark Twain knew that to teach, one must also entertain. He always made his readers laugh. Many said this was all he did, but they were not reading closely. "Humor," wrote Mark Twain in his *Autobiography,* "is only a fragrance, a decoration. Often it is merely an odd trick of speech and spelling . . . and presently the fashion passes and the fame along with it. There are those who say a novel should be a work of art solely and you must not preach in it, you must not teach in it. That may be true as regards novels but it is not true as regards humor. Humor must not professedly teach and it must not professedly preach, but it must do both if it would live forever."

Well, he did both, and there is little doubt that his books will live so long as there is one young boy or girl left in the world who wants to go down the Mississippi or to the Court of King Arthur and to laugh with Mark Twain as he gets himself a Genuine Mexican Plug. The boy becomes a man and the girl a woman, and they both still go back to Sam Clemens's books because he has made a world within in them that captures our hearts, enriches our minds, and expands our horizons.